THE SILENCE OF SUMMERLAND

Ruth McQuillan-Wilson

Published by and copyright © 2023 Lily Publications (IOM) Ltd.

All rights reserved.

ISBN 978-1-91177-93-7

The rights of Ruth McQuillan-Wilson to be identified as the author of this work have been asserted in accordance with the Copyright Act 1991.

For Mum and Dad,
who loved the Isle of Man with
all their hearts; just as I do.

Contents

"The past is a foreign country; they do things differently there."

The Go-Between, by L.P. Hartley

Preamble

Sammy, Muriel, Ruth and Lynda went to the Isle of Man in 1973. It was their first family holiday across the water. A dream was beginning to come true, then a terrible thing happened. Their lives, and the lives of many others, changed on the evening of 2nd August. They grieved for the people who were lost, although they didn't know them. Friendships were forged through tragedy.

Years went by. A crust formed over the wound, but it was unable to heal. The event was rarely spoken of, and the silence caused it to ache. It felt as if it had been forgotten; yet it never gave up hope that a time would come when it would be examined again – a time to talk.

Introduction

The sun shines from a clear blue sky, and birds sing sweetly in trees laden with foliage. There is an abundance of green, even though it never rains. Bees hum around pretty flowers and other little creatures scurry back and forth through luscious grass, safe from harm.

Everyone is smiling. There are funfairs, candy floss and trips to the beach, where gentle waves lap the shore, and parents watch contentedly while children play.

Those images would have filled my five-year-old mind if I'd known, in advance of our August holiday, that we would be going to a place called Summerland. I was an imaginative child, and during my first year at primary school I was gently chastised for letting my thoughts wander far beyond the infant classroom. The final weeks of term were devoted to daydreams of our upcoming trip and the big boat that would carry us across the Irish Sea. I had never been on a boat before, and I communicated my excitement to anyone who would listen!

The sun wasn't shining when we arrived in Douglas, but the damp, grey day did not lower our spirits, and we managed to build sandcastles between the showers. It was wonderful to be in the relaxed, friendly atmosphere of the beautiful Isle of Man.

My father realised one of his dreams in Summerhill Glen, when he watched two little pairs of eyes, one brown and the other blue, light up with joy. He had spoken to us often about the "fairy glen," and the great day had come at last.

I didn't want to leave that peaceful haven, but arrangements had been made to meet relatives in Summerland. They were several days into their holiday and had been waiting for us at the docks. During the short drive to our boarding house, the adults chatted about the evening ahead and the forecast of further rain. A venue was suggested which seemed ideal.

The little worm of anxiety that had been furrowing my brow as we approached Summerland[1] vanished when we entered the building. I think of the moment my young senses absorbed the spectacular sights and sounds of the Island's new entertainment centre as my *Charlie and the Chocolate Factory* experience.[2]

Everything was bright and colourful! It didn't matter that the waterfall wasn't gushing liquid chocolate. There were eye-catching stalls full of sweets, ice cream and other treats waiting to be enjoyed. Signposts indicated further delights, downstairs. Hobby horses were a particular favourite of mine, and I was keen to have a ride on the carousel.

Our time in Summerland was to be brief, however. While thousands of people were being entertained inside, three Liverpool schoolboys had spied something that interested them in a corner of the outdoor terrace.

A fibreglass hut, previously used as a pay kiosk for the crazy golf, had suffered storm damage at the start of the season. All but one section had been carried off to a storeroom after it was taken apart.

Perhaps those responsible for the task were called away to do something else, and it was forgotten about. Maybe it was glanced at every now and then, causing the observer to make a mental note to attend to it later; but like so many things in life, no one ever got round to it.[3]

The abandoned part lay on its side. If anyone had looked in, they may have seen some wind-borne litter and the remainder of a plastic covered roll of wire netting. The Liverpool boy had matches. A fire started.[4]

Summerland staff made valiant efforts to quench the blaze at the eastern end of the sea-facing wall, which had been clad with Galbestos. Fire extinguishers and a hose, passed through a window in the amusement arcade, made no impact. The battle was one they could not win. During the struggle to move the burning kiosk away from the building, it collapsed against the wall, and a fire began to develop in the void behind the cladding.[5]

In the confusion, no one called the fire brigade. This didn't happen until more than twenty minutes after the kiosk fire started. Emergency services had already been alerted by sources outside the centre. By the time a distressed manager rang for help, Summerland's fate was sealed.[6]

Vapour fuelled flames roared into the amusement arcade when the Decalin, that lined the other side of the void, was defeated.[7] Gaps at the end of each terrace created a chimney effect, drawing death towards men, women and children on the upper floors, who, only moments before, had been taking in a show, relaxing in the Sundome, playing games or just walking about, savouring the atmosphere.[8] A wall of flame, steadily increasing in stature, surged from the arcade. To those on the flying staircase, it must have felt as if their "last hour had come."[9]

In its death throes, Summerland's Solarium wept molten tears on its patrons as they fled for their lives.[10]

∗∗∗

Tendrils of smoke, drifting into the building, had been forerunners of disaster. Advice not to panic meant that some people lingered, and a number, who had begun to leave, went back to their seats. My father spotted smoke coming from an air vent and was uneasy about it. We were on the top floor, having gone there to begin our Summerland adventure. He was a man who usually listened to authority, but the voice of intuition, clamouring for attention, was impossible to ignore. It was time for us to go.

As Dad led us down the flying staircase, smoke was sneaking through the open treads, winding around ankles and lower legs. When we turned onto a landing, which lead to the final flight, the building erupted in flames. It seemed as if our little family was doomed.

Dad looked about in despair. He was on the point of urging us to retrace our steps – it appeared to be the only option – when he discovered that Mum and I were no longer behind him. Just then, he spied a door that had given way, twisted by the heat. With two-year-old Lynda in his arms, hair on fire and his jacket melting into his back, he made a run for it.[11]

At the end of the outdoor terrace, a man standing on the concrete steps – some four feet from the top – called out to my father, urging him to throw the baby down. The kind stranger held up his arms, ready to receive the terrified toddler when Dad dropped her to safety. Lynda's forehead was burnt, and there were raw patches on her little bare legs. With a last look at his precious daughter, Dad turned away. Skin had peeled off his cheeks and nose, and there were burns on his hands too. Oblivious to his injuries, he returned to the blazing building to search for the other half of his world.

The heat was beyond description. Strong arms held him back. In the gentlest way possible, he was told there was no hope; that Summerland was no longer a place compatible with life.

My parents and sister were gone. My desperate attempts to cling on to daddy's coat tail were futile; I wasn't strong enough. I couldn't prevent the bond from being broken.

The stampeding crowd swallowed me in a frantic retreat to the upper floors, where death must surely claim us! Long legs, some in flared trousers, blocked my view. Smoke stung my eyes. Then I saw her: my mummy. The first call was inaudible, choked by fear. I tried again. She heard me and turned. The terror of what might happen was written plainly on her face. She struggled to stay upright. One of the hardest things in the world is to go against the crowd. With a mother's love, she fought, her strength superhuman, fuelled by her child's petrified cries. I was burning. Red-hot flames lashed little limbs. Adrenalin numbed the pain. We were reunited. She was burnt too.

When I emerged from the ruins, I was a different person: changed both physically and emotionally. The more outspoken among my contemporaries were keen to comment on the former. Summerland was not discussed in our house. Relatives and close friends avoided the subject. At times, however, a question was asked by someone outside our family, usually about the origin of my scars. I hated that. I wanted to be the same as everyone else. I concealed my injuries as much as possible. I didn't want to be questioned, especially when I didn't have the answers. I avoided situations in which my secret might be uncovered. When I heard the name *Isle of Man*, I felt ill.

I also felt guilty because I had survived, when so many others lost their lives.

After my father passed away, at the end of 2007, I was tormented by panic attacks, nightmares and flashbacks. A confrontation with Summerland could no longer be avoided. Desperation drove me to research the event that had drastically changed my life.[12]

I discovered the names of the fifty men, women and children whose presence I had felt since I was five years old. I read them aloud, my voice breaking with emotion. I thought of the other people who were injured, eighty or more, and wondered how their lives had been.

Realisation dawned swiftly. My Summerland journey was not over. It had only just begun.

***

I stood before the derelict Summerland site, trembling, on a day that felt surreal. It was a wet Thursday, in May 2012, like that fateful one nearly thirty-nine years before. I felt a heavy weight on my shoulders. There was something I needed to do, but how? I was a stranger on the Isle of Man. I had barely slept in the weeks before my trip, so great was my fear. Then I remembered something. On the rare occasions when the subject of Summerland was raised, my parents never spoke with bitterness. My father referred to the fire as a tragic accident, and my mother told people about the friendly Manx folk and of the great kindness shown to us. They recalled a wonderful honeymoon in 1962, during which they were treated as part of the family by the proprietors of a Douglas boarding house. A flicker of hope gave me courage.

Two years after I confronted my "demon," I travelled to the Island alone. My week in Douglas was a maelstrom of emotions. It wasn't easy to speak of the past, and I cried on the shoulders of many local people. In fact, for the most part, we cried together. I made new friends, and for the first time in my life I had a sense of belonging. I realised that, quite incredibly, Douglas had begun to feel like home. I understood, at last, my father's affinity with the Isle of Man, and why he so desperately wanted to share its beauty and inimitable character with those dearest to him. My greatest regret is that we were unable to experience the magic together in my adult life.

I wish we had been able to get beyond the silence of Summerland, when we still had the chance. The end came too quickly and so much was left unsaid. There was nothing I could do to change that, but I hoped that by talking openly about the tragedy others would be encouraged to speak about it. I believed that increased awareness would prevent errors, which weren't evident at the time of the building's construction, from occurring again.[13] How I wished that with that with every fibre of my being. It was unbearable to think of further lives being torn apart. I convinced myself that a fire like the one at Summerland couldn't happen in modern times. I had to, in order to carry on!

Chapter 1: Fastyr Mie
(Good afternoon or good evening)

I hate saying farewell to Douglas. The weather is often glorious on my last day, which makes the pain of separation worse. The colours are never brighter or the call of the gull more keen, than during those final moments. I can barely look at the shimmering waves when the taxi pulls out to join the stream of traffic. In summer, the steady clip-clop of a horse tram taunts me as we drive along the promenade. It is usually full of holidaymakers, travelling the other way.

***

My greeting to the "little people" came seconds before that of the taxi driver, when we crossed the Fairy Bridge over the Santon Burn. I thought of the changes in my life since I first saluted the mooinjer veggey. Back then, I knew no one on the Island. Its people, special places and customs were unfamiliar.

All too soon, we reached Ballasalla, where the words *Airport Garage* on a forecourt canopy, proclaimed the journey's imminent end, causing my heart to ache.

I spotted Jamie immediately. He was sitting on one of the seats in front of the check-in desks, where I often sit for a while, to compose myself, before going upstairs. I've never seen more than a few people waiting there, unlike other airports where the reception area is usually a hive of activity. Perhaps people are reluctant to leave the beautiful Isle of Man and delay their journey to the airport as much as possible. I have erred on the side of caution since almost missing a flight in 2014, after squeezing the very last drop of pleasure from my autumn trip.

It was lovely to see a familiar face at Ronaldsway and to have a brief chat. Although we'd only met the night before, Jamie and I shared a bond already: the bond of Summerland.

Sometime later, I saw Jamie again; his flight had just been called. I watched him join the queue of people London bound and was eager for the Belfast flight to be announced; for the limbo of departures to be over.

Finally, my turn came. I always enjoyed watching the short safety video during which Manx children demonstrated the procedures to be implemented in the case of an emergency. The safety demonstrations on other airlines fill me with fear, and I know that if the worst were to happen, I wouldn't remember any of the instructions.

Most of my journeys to the Isle of Man occurred before noon. After boarding the little nineteen-seater plane, I eagerly awaited the children's cheery greeting of *moghrey mie* at the start of the video. It was always a good morning when I was travelling to Mona's Isle.

Although the same video was shown on Citywing flights when noon had been and gone, the Manx greeting, given then, indicated that the day was no longer young.

The line dividing afternoon from evening was blurred when we took off. I thought of Jamie, home now as I soon would be, and of the days ahead; days in which we both had a task to complete.

Chapter 2: The Road to the Sloc
(Sloc: a pit, dip or hollow)

Search lovely Mona's Isle through,
You'll find no such enchanting view,
As Rushen vale in summer hue,
From the cottage in the heather.

When I saw the memorial to *Tom the Dipper*, I knew we were on the right road.[14]

A Manx friend had taken me to visit the monument on a beautiful August day in 2015, just a short time after I arrived on the Isle of Man. The peaceful setting, above the village of Ballakilpheric, was soothing after the stress of the journey. Thankfully, I am much more relaxed about flying now; although, I'll never forget how petrified I was during my first flight to the Island as an adult. It took every bit of determination I possessed to make that trip.

Three stone steps lead to a well-kept patch of green, where the stone memorial nestles in the grass. As well as extolling the incredible view, the inscription informs the reader that Tom's cottage once sat there. A dwelling he built with the assistance of his wife Nell and generously bequeathed to the poor.

Thomas Shimmin was a ragman by trade. As well as his name, a sign on his cart bore the words, "True Manninagh": True Manxman – a declaration of his proud heritage!

In his rag gathering days, Thomas and his trusty donkey set off each morning from their base in Port Erin. While they went about their business, the donkey was probably thinking about his next meal, but Thomas was revelling in the beauty surrounding him and composing poetry in his mind. One of the events that inspired

Thomas, was the foundering of the brig, *Lily*. After reading his account of the tragedy, I decided to find out more about the ill-fated ship.

***

Destined for the west coast of Africa, the *Lily* departed from Liverpool with an extensive cargo on board. Among the goods she was transporting, were cotton, cloth bales and rum. Also, in the hold during that direful voyage in December 1852, were cannon, guns and barrels of gunpowder.

Extreme weather had wreaked havoc from the penultimate Friday of the year; and battered vessels, flotsam and debris strewn beaches around the Isle of Man, told a sorry tale of the perilous conditions at sea. A lifeboat, the *British Queen*, became the latest casualty, when, on the twenty-seventh day of the month, she ran aground at Castletown (the Island's capital at that time). The storm, however, had not finished its rampage, and the lifeboat would not be its last victim that day.

The *Lily*, owned by Messrs Hatton and Cookson, was borne back by the tide from the coast of Ireland, much scarred from her struggle with the weather. She found shelter in the Sound, near the Calf of Man, where the "Drinking Dragon" will forever gaze upon the magical kingdom beneath the waves.[15]

Just a short time after setting sail again, the unfortunate brig was caught in the grip of the strong current. The tremendous efforts made by her crew, to avoid disaster, were in vain. They could not prevent the *Lily* from striking Kitterland, an islet in the Sound.

***

Sometime before I learned of the Liverpool brig's sad demise, I'd come upon the legend of Baron Kitter, who owned a castle on the summit of Barrule.It seems the Norwegian was a voracious hunter, and soon no bison or elk remained on the Isle of Man. Terrified that the blood-thirsty baron would begin to slay their own animals, the people sought help from the Island's shrewdest witches. Witch Ada obliged by casting a spell. It caused the pot that Eaoch, the Baron's cook, had fallen asleep in front of to spew its fatty contents into the flames. It wasn't long before the whole place was burning.

Eaoch, known for his loud voice, was roused from his slumber by the calamity that had befallen his master's home. He shrieked with all his might. Although Kitter and his friends were far away on the Calf of Man, pursuing deer, they heard the terrified cries. When the Baron looked towards the Island and saw the blaze, he took off for the beach in great alarm. He was closely followed by his comrades. They all jumped into a small vessel and set sail. However, it seems as if the current had conspired with Witch Ada to bring about the baron's demise. The boat collided with a "rock" in the Sound, between the Calf and the main island. There were no survivors, and from that moment on the islet was known as Kitterland.[16]

***

Despite the thrashing of men and brig by wind and waves, a jolly boat was launched. In this, the crew of the *Lily* made it to the rocks at Kitterland. Most of them managed to clamber onto the islet, but several poor shivering wretches did not.

Captain John failed to gain purchase when he jumped from a narrow ledge. Three members of his crew – an orphan lad among them – also lost their tenuous grip on the slippery surface. The life of the ship's carpenter was claimed by the foremast, when it came crashing down.

The safety of the sailors on Kitterland was not guaranteed. Gigantic waves crashed over the islet, where the exhausted men must have felt doomed.

A woman from Cregneash, who had been walking along the cliff, witnessed the shocking scene and ran to tell her brother. He set off with great speed to Port St Mary, in search of a boat of sufficient size to carry out a rescue mission. A yawl was transported by cart to the Sound, where the brave Manxmen, who had readily volunteered for the task, put to sea despite the treacherous conditions.

They succeeded in bringing the *Lily's* survivors to safety. One crew member – the second mate – had suffered a serious injury to his leg, and the journey to Port St Mary must have been agony for him. Though, once there, the kindly locals were on hand to offer comfort and tend to his needs, and to those of the other survivors.

In the wake of the terrible fire at Summerland, Douglas residents rushed to the aid of its victims. Hundreds of Manx people responded to a radio appeal for blood donors and queued for hours in the hope of saving a life. Homes were opened to the relatives and friends of the bereaved and injured, when they arrived on the Island consumed by worry and grief. Local families, full of compassion, consoled and cared for the poor souls, many of whom had the most awful task imaginable ahead of them.

There would be another catastrophic event in the Sound, the day after the *Lily's* foundering, which would cause sorrow and hardship for many in the area. Indeed, it would leave few families untouched.

***

The *Lily's* insurers placed responsibility for the vessel and her cargo into the hands of one of their sub-agents, Mr Lace, from Port St Mary – a man who wore more than one hat in his daily life. He contacted the Lloyds' agent in Douglas, and a plan was formed. The team who would protect the cargo and see it safely brought to shore, included police constables from Castletown (one was the chief constable) and a constable from Port St Mary. The moon was bright that night. Storm clouds scurried across its face on their way to cause mayhem elsewhere.

In the calm of early Tuesday morning – calm before another kind of storm during which horrendous deaths and utter destruction would occur – a band of men left their homes and families and set off for Kitterland.

The cliffs seemed to rise to greater heights behind those who began their journey across the cold, dark water of the Sound as if trying to shelter them from harm. But when the boat pulled away from shore, they diminished with each sweep of the oars. Nothing could protect the men from their fate, just a short distance away.

A number of casks of gunpowder had been discovered, washed up, at Port Erin; but the *Lily* still held some forty tons when she sat upon the rocks, where the tide had left her, patiently awaiting the volunteers.

An acrid smell lingered about the brig, worrying the men, but the first part of the recovery went smoothly. Though, when dawn broke a sinister sight was revealed. Most of the salvagers were keen to abandon the ship because of the gunpowder in the hold; but were persuaded to proceed, as it seemed that the billows of smoke weren't coming from where it was stored. To establish the location of the fire, a hole was made in the deck. The intention was to tip water through it to quench the flames, but fresh morning air rushed in first…

At around 8:00 am on 28th December, a massive explosion rocked the south of the Isle of Man. Many residents felt sure it was an earthquake. Miners at Ballacorkish were flung to the ground, and the mine was plunged into darkness when candles were snuffed out by the shock, which incredibly was felt in homes in Douglas and beyond.

Part of a watch, worn by one of the victims of the blast, was later found three miles away. More distressing evidence of the devastation was discovered five miles from the explosion. Even the ship's ironmongery had been torn asunder.

Men on the shore, who had been watching the launch of a second boat of volunteers, stood rooted to the spot when disaster struck. The very caps had been swept from their heads. Their gaze was fixed on the space occupied by the Liverpool brig and the salvage team, just moments before. Smoke was slowly clearing, and as the truth was revealed voices were raised in horror.

How torturous for the wives, mothers and children with loved ones on Kitterland that day. I can picture them wringing their hands in anguish, longing for news, yet dreading it at the same time, a gut-wrenching wait. Then it came, turning their blood to ice and sapping the strength from their limbs. It tore out their hearts and stamped on hope, but hope is hard to extinguish. For one family, a tiny glimmer remained, a fragile thing that would require careful tending. It promised nothing; it couldn't, but its existence meant everything to them.

James Kelly sustained horrific injuries in the explosion. When the inquiry into the tragedy got underway, his life was hanging in the balance. Although he hadn't been on the brig when the explosion occurred, James lost consciousness because of the sheer force. Finding himself unable to see or hear, when he finally came round, he began to wash his face in what he believed to be a pool of water. It wasn't water; it was blood.

Miraculously, James, from Port St Mary, recovered from his terrifying ordeal, though he lost one of his ears and a large area of flesh from his cheek. His dear wife, Margaret, died in 1877. She was just fifty-one; James outlived her by almost fourteen years. He worked extremely hard every day of his life. He passed away, aged sixty-eight, nearly four decades after the tragedy. I am sure he relived it in his mind many, many times. His position was a lonely one. A beautifully carved headstone (erected by their son) marks the grave James shares with Margaret. Along the bottom of it, are thirteen words and a date: a declaration that he was the sole survivor at Kitterland on that dreadful day.

An arched memorial at Kirk Christ, Rushen, bears the names of the twenty-nine brave men who died trying to save the *Lily's* cargo. It states that they "lost their lives" as does the original memorial in the Kaye Garden, Douglas, say of the fifty victims of the Summerland fire. More than twenty-two years passed before the tribute to the Manxmen was erected by Mr Quillam, from the Castletown Marble Works, by request of "The Kitterland Explosion Fund" committee. The first memorial to the Summerland victims, was thoughtfully erected by Douglas Borough Council on the twenty-fifth anniversary of the disaster.

The surname Callister appears five times on the brig *Lily* memorial. Four men bearing the name Watterson perished, while the Gale family lost three of their loved ones.

Twenty-three of those who died in the 1852 tragedy, including the Castletown constables, shared one of the following first names: Edward, John, Thomas and William. Three of these, are the first or second names of several of the men who died in Summerland, obviously just as popular the following century. Of the remaining six forenames on the monument, in the grounds of the Rushen parish church, two appear on the Summerland memorial as middle names. One of the others is particularly close to my heart: Samuel, the name of my own dear dad, who did everything in his power to make our childhood happy after the fire.

The name William Cowley immediately stood out to me. In 2018, I contacted some of the brave firemen who fought the inferno at Summerland. It was something I'd wanted to do for many years, and a Manx friend helped to fulfil my wish. I received a reply to every letter I sent. One of the gentlemen who responded is named William Cowley!

Twenty-two women were widowed by the tragedy in the Sound, and seventy-seven children were left fatherless. Among those who died, were carpenters, fishermen and a publican. The Castletown constables also left widows and young families. Without the breadwinner, many families were destitute.

Church collections were the only source of aid for the Island's poor, at that time; and a collection was made on the Sunday following the explosion, but more help was needed. A fund for the widows and orphans of the disaster was established in Liverpool as well as the Isle of Man. People gave generously. Mr E.M. Gawne Esq., captain of the parish of Rushen, known for his munificence, donated £100. He became one of the fund's trustees, ably assisted by the vicar and the curate. Donations on the adjacent isle included sums from a gunpowder factory and a company that manufactured safes. The Reverend Hugh Stowell Brown (renowned for his contribution to social reform) – brother of Manx Poet, T.E. Brown – handed over the proceeds of one of his talks. There was even a donation from Queen Victoria and Prince Albert. The *Liverpool Mercury* reported on the progress of the fund.

The Summerland disaster fund was also extremely well supported, by people of all ages, on the Isle of Man and in the United Kingdom. Douglas Corporation and the Isle of Man Government started the ball rolling with generous donations. Summerland's surviving staff members held a concert and gave the proceeds to the fund. One lady remembers that cuddly toys, which escaped the ravages of the fire, were given as raffle prizes. Everything possible was done to support the victims and their families.

In the days after the fire disaster, the newspapers were full of reports about the tragedy. Heart breaking stories appeared in papers throughout the British Isles. News of the catastrophic event even made it into the *New York Times*.

The tragedy at the Sound, more than a century earlier, was reported to the *London Illustrated News* by a Castletown resident. A drawing in that same paper, published on 8th January 1853, shows the calamitous scene. It almost looks as if a volcano is erupting from the sea. A black cloud, like that which rose above Summerland (and could be seen for miles), looms over Kitterland, and fragments of the brig are clearly visible among the flames.

At the bottom of the memorial to those who perished in the dreadful explosion in 1852, are the following words: *In the Midst of Life We Are in Death*, from *The Book of Common Prayer*. They are words that I think of often because of the truth that is in them.[17]

∗∗∗

After spotting the monument to benevolent poet, singer and Baptist preacher, Thomas Shimmin, in November 2016, I relaxed a little. After just one wrong turn, we arrived at our destination: the home of a gentleman who is a fluent Manx Gaelic speaker: a "True Manninagh!" The scenery stole my breath away, and I envied anyone able to wake up to such an incredible view every morning. It struck me as the perfect retreat for writers and artists: peaceful, unspoilt and with more than a hint of isolation. In today's busy world, in which housing estates spring up where animals once grazed and wildflowers grew, I can think of nothing more wonderful than a little house near the Sloc.

My host also had a flight to catch, just a few hours after mine, but he welcomed me into his home as if he had all the time in the world.

In messages before our meeting, I'd mentioned some of the Manx myths and legends that enthral me. One of my favourites is the tale of the vampire of Malew[18] (a parish in the south of the Island).

In October 2014, when I travelled to the Isle of Man to celebrate Hop tu naa,[19] I was collected at the airport by a Manx friend who took me to see the "vampire's" grave. The four iron stakes, and the chains fixed to them, called to mind horror films I'd watched in my youth. My favourites featured Bram Stoker's *Dracula*. Even though they terrified me, I found them compelling and watched them again and again!

THE SILENCE OF SUMMERLAND

When it was time to leave my cosy surroundings, I asked if I should go out through the back door, as I'd gone to the front one, in error, when I arrived. I should have known better. My grandparents and parents-in-law were all country dwellers. The front door was only used during two events, one happy and the other sad. The kitchen, after all, is the heart of the home, and they used the door that brought them directly to it. I was surprised to be told no – I should leave the way I came in or the luck would go from the house. I treasured that little gem and thought of it often.

On a dark November evening, two years later, it seemed that luck had not only left my home but deserted me completely.

Chapter 3: "Travelling in the Dusk"
(*The Deemster*, by Hall Caine)

Darkness was falling as we made our way to the airport. Lights were on in many of the houses we passed, and several sitting room windows were already adorned for the forthcoming festive season. At Ronaldsway, I thanked the taxi driver, who had taken me to the Sloc, when he wished me well at the end of our little adventure. The first company I called had declined my request because they didn't know the area. Then, one of the hotel reception staff suggested a different firm. When the taxi arrived, I explained to the driver that I wasn't entirely sure where we were going. Neither was he, but he responded to the challenge enthusiastically. We said goodbye, and I reluctantly left the warmth of the car. My reluctance though, had more to do with the fact that my lovely holiday was over than the coolness of the air.

When I climbed the stairs after completing check-in, I was delighted to see an array of Christmas "trees" of different shapes and sizes. Each one was imaginatively decorated. Earlier in the week, I'd discovered that the Christmas lights were being switched on in Douglas, just a few hours after my flight home, and I wished that I had planned my trip more thoughtfully.

The Save the Children's *Festival of Trees* display was a lovely surprise. Visitors to the airport could vote for their favourite when the event opened. A tree covered with little life jackets (I later found out it was called *Refutree*) caught my eye, but in fact, they were all magnificent and represented many hours of dedicated work.

The theme for the Isle of Man Post Office's contribution that year was *The Wizard of Oz*.[20] From beneath a post box strung with little lights and festooned with *letters*, the wicked witch's legs, clad in striped stockings, poked out. The red bulbs were reflected in shoes of the same colour on the lifeless feet – the famous ruby slippers! A windswept *Toto* was perched in his basket on top of the box, and in the background, an illuminated yellow brick road stretched all the way to a twinkling Emerald City.

I was reminded of a tough decision when I was a child. *The Wizard of Oz* seemed to be shown on television at the same time as *Peter Pan*[21] in the Christmas holidays. Both were films I thoroughly enjoyed. Peter often rescued me during sleepless nights after the fire. He would take me to places far away from my dark bedroom, where flames flickered on the walls when the light was switched off. Dorothy Gale was an inspiration, proof that good *can* overcome evil! The scarecrow was terrified of fire, just as I was, and like me, the lion wanted to be brave.

It would be very difficult to choose a winner I thought, as I took a last look at the wonderful creations.

The final morning of my November trip had been spent shopping for gifts. The cards bought earlier in the week, were already on their way to homes in Northern Ireland and the adjacent isle. I'd wondered, when I posted them, if their recipients would be surprised by the Manx Christmas stamps. Though, by then, my deep love for the Isle of Man was well known among family and friends.

Unable to buy all the things I wanted due to weight restrictions, I vowed to check in a second bag when booking my next flight. I have shopped in many towns, but there is nowhere quite like Douglas. It has a wonderful atmosphere all year round.

Among my purchases, were a novel and a cuddly penguin with a string of colourful lights around its plump middle. As soon as I saw *Doolie*, a story began to form in my mind. The little hero of *Christmas Lights* sits proudly on my daughter's shelf; a reminder of a better time in my life: a time when I was able to travel without difficulty, to the little island that means so much to me.

In the departure lounge at Ronaldsway Airport, I studied the blurb on my Manx Classics edition of *The Deemster*.[22] I was amazed to learn that the story had been published in more than nine different languages across fifty editions. It was so popular that readers travelled to the Isle of Man to see some of the places mentioned in the book.

King Edward VII and his Queen, Alexandra, visited the Island at the beginning of the new century. Both thoroughly enjoyed Caine's novels and were eager to see the Manx settings themselves. Caine, an MHK,[23] was a cordial host, and he received an invitation to have dinner with the Royal couple on board their yacht.

Hall Caine was somewhat of a celebrity in his day. Remarkably, he was even recognised when far from home. Crowds of fans swarmed to greet him during a trip to New York, where he was accompanied by his wife and son!

Caine's schooldays came to an end when he was fourteen, but he continued to study, worked extremely hard and grasped every opportunity. He overcame illness and fought against grief more than once in his life. As I delved further for information, I discovered, to my delight, the friendship between Hall Caine and Dublin born Bram Stoker!

I can identify with Abraham (Bram) Stoker, the younger, as he too spent lengthy periods confined to bed as a child. In the long, solitary hours, the little boy had plenty of time to think; and later in his life he put those thoughts to good use. Thankfully, Bram recovered by the age of seven.

Bram Stoker, like Caine, was inspired by his surroundings, the people he met and tales he'd heard from family members and acquaintances. In 1897, his famous novel *Dracula*, which he dedicated to his "Dear Friend Hommy-Beg," was published. I enjoy it even more now that I'm aware of the connection between the two men.[24]

Thomas Henry *Hall* Caine, who had a Manx father and an English mother, was born on 14th May 1853, in Runcorn, Cheshire, where his father had a temporary job at the docks. When John

Caine, a blacksmith, travelled to Liverpool from his island home, in search of employment, he spent further time training. This enabled him to secure smithing work on the ships. Sarah Hall, a seamstress, had moved to the city, from Cumberland, with her family – who could trace their Quaker heritage back many generations. John was an Anglican, and although Sarah may have stopped attending meetings of the Society of Friends after their marriage, her upbringing was forever evident in her demeanour and attire.

Not long after baby Thomas (Caine preferred to be called Hall due to his dislike of the name Thomas) was born, the new little family of three moved back to the city, where they lived in rented accommodation close to the docks: an area inhabited by other Manx folk. Several moves followed, and five more children were born.

Tragedy struck the Caine family when Hall was nine years old. In just twelve months, two of his sisters passed away. Sarah was only five when hydrocephaly, following a fever, brought about her demise. Baby Emma contracted whooping cough, which her brothers, Hall and John had been suffering from. Convulsions claimed the little girl's life. Plans were made for the eldest boy to return to the land of his father's birth to recuperate.

Grief-stricken after the loss of his sisters, and much weakened by illness, the youngster, with a label attached to his jacket, was dispatched to the Isle of Man. His uncle had arranged to meet the boat in Ramsey. However, there would be further tribulation to be endured before the boy reached safe harbour and the loving arms of his Manx relatives. A terrible storm necessitated the rescue of the ferry's passengers. A big rowing boat brought the frightened and weary travellers ashore. It was an experience that Caine would later recall and use in one of his Manx novels.

The young lad began his recovery at his grandmother's cosy cottage in Ballaugh. He learned of the Island's myths and legends: tales of witchcraft, the "evil eye," etc, while they sat by the hearth gazing into the flames. The good lady endearingly called her grandson "Hommy-Beg" – "Little Tommy" – and further enriched his knowledge of Manx culture and folklore each time he stayed with her.

Hall lost his maternal grandfather when he was seventeen. Ralph's death was a dreadful blow. The two formed a close bond after Sarah's parents moved in with the family when the children were young. Around the time of his grandfather's passing, Hall began to suffer from bouts of anxiety. These would continue to trouble him throughout the rest of his life. He quit his employment and travelled to the Isle of Man, where he took up the role of assistant to his schoolmaster uncle James Teare, who had tuberculosis. His Manx grandmother – Isabella – had passed away several years previously.

The home of his Uncle James and Aunt Catherine (his father's sister) in Maughold, which was part of the schoolhouse, was already cramped before Hall arrived to swell the ranks. It was simply not big enough to accommodate everyone, so Hall decided to make a home of his own in a rundown cottage. Work that he was able to undertake himself thanks to Ralph's tutelage. The tholtan was soon habitable. As a finishing touch, the talented teenager carved the name he had given it above the door. His new dwelling, completed in January 1871, was called Phoenix Cottage.

The relaxed way of life on the beautiful Isle of Man suited Hall Caine. When James Teare was defeated by his illness, Hall carved a headstone for the grave and became schoolmaster in his uncle's place. As well as teaching duties, Caine, always an avid reader and keen writer, helped local people make their wills, fill out documents and even write letters to loved ones, the way his uncle had done. James had been very encouraging about his nephew's ability as a writer, which led to him submitting articles to a local newspaper on a variety of subjects. This, he did anonymously.

Unfortunately, the idyllic life on the Island ended abruptly. Hall was summoned back to Liverpool by the gentleman he'd been apprenticed to at the age of fifteen. Architect, John Murray, believed that the young man's talents would be put to better use there. Indeed, he contributed articles to publications concerned with the building trade that were well received.

So keen was Hall Caine to have his work published, that he wrote theatre reviews for newspapers free of charge. His talent did not go unnoticed; and in his journalistic career he rose to the position of "leader-writer" for the *Liverpool Mercury*.

Caine had many distinguished friends, including Dante Gabriel Rossetti and Sir Henry Irving. He met Sir Henry, actor-manager at the Lyceum Theatre, in his capacity as theatre critic. Irving was very impressed by Hall's review of his performance in William Shakespeare's Hamlet – Sir Henry played the protagonist. They continued to correspond, and introductions were made. Irving's business manager also had the writing bug. His name was Bram Stoker!

Hall Caine outlived his good friend Stoker – who composed an introduction to one of the later editions of *The Deemster* – by almost two decades, and when he passed away at Greeba Castle in 1931, was buried on that dear island which had become his permanent home. Greeba, a castellated structure rather than a castle, had been rented by Caine while writing one of his novels: *The Manxman*. When the book was published, he was able to buy and make changes to the house with some of the proceeds. Greeba Castle's designer, a Douglas man, who had become an architect under his own steam, was responsible for a number of other buildings of a "castellated" design. Summerland's predecessor, Derby Castle, was one of them!

I've read two accounts of where Sir Hall Caine wrote *The Deemster*. When I think of him, it is not beneath the soil at Kirk Maughold or on the Greeba Estate. I picture him sitting at a table in a Douglas Boarding House, the plot unfolding on the pages before him, completely unaware of how popular the book would be!

Douglas was changing. The Palace Pavilion, with its huge ballroom, opened in 1887, the year of the novel's publication, and a chair lift was installed to carry holidaymakers to Falcon Cliff, high above the promenade. That popular venue also benefited from the addition of a large dance hall at the end of the decade. The Victorian holidaymakers, who flocked to the Island's capital, were spoilt for choice. (Caine even wrote a guide book for the Isle of Man Steam Packet Company.)

Nearly one hundred and thirty years after Hall Caine travelled to the Isle of Man, to spend time in the locations that would feature in *The Deemster*, I sat in my hotel writing *Made in Summerland*.[25] Every now and then, I'd look across the bay or along the promenade towards the memorial garden, at its northern end; wherein the statue stands of a man whose torch of success burned brightly during his lifetime. Some places of entertainment, which were in their heyday in the author's time, are gone now; but I see them clearly in my mind's eye, ready to greet visitors old and new. Many who come to Ellan Vannin will leave their hearts behind, just as I did, in dear old Doolish by the sea.[26]

After drinking in every word on *The Deemster's* cover and relishing the multitude of crisp new pages in between, I tucked it down the side of my bag; unwilling to be disturbed by the call to board just as I was getting into the story. It would be quite some months before I became acquainted with the book's characters. When I did eventually invite them into my life, I quickly realised that they would stay with me forever.

Finally installed on the Belfast flight, I settled back and thought about my trip. I was determined to learn Manx Gaelic. In fact, I couldn't wait to begin; but when I did manage to make a start, life put another obstacle in my way.

***

Across the Island, glittering lights, like numerous eyes, seemed to watch as we climbed into the evening sky. Several seats on the plane were empty, including the one next to me. In the absence of someone to talk to, my mind went back to the chat I'd had earlier about Manannan Mac Lir.

I've been fascinated by Manannan since I was introduced to him by a friendly taxi driver in 2012, when I travelled to the Isle of Man to visit the derelict Summerland site and confront the past. I was delighted with the notion that the son of the sea spreads his cloak of invisibility over the Island, in the form of a thick mist, to protect it from harm; and listened attentively, while the Manxman elaborated.

I had no idea, until 2015, that Manannan is a god in Irish mythology too, even though I've been familiar with the legends of warrior heroes, Fionn Mac Cumhaill (Finn McCool) and Cu Chulainn, since childhood.

Manannan's impressive possessions include a powerful sword: The *Answerer* (*Fragarach*), which can slice through armour, and a breastplate capable of withstanding every assault. *Enbarr* carries his master over land and sea with ease; his magnificent mane streaming in the wind as he gallops along. *Wave Sweeper*, the sea god's mystical chariot, has no need for sail or oars. The enchanted vessel knows its master's wishes without a word being spoken.

In bygone days, Manannan, who bestowed his name on the Island, came to the aid of the Manx people with incredible speed. When alien fleets were approaching, he changed into a three-legged shape and cart-wheeled down the mountainside. Using illusions, Manannan made it look as if many battle ships were waiting to confront the would-be invaders, who soon beat a hasty retreat. He could also trick enemies into thinking that a single man was a multitude, thus staving off trouble and preserving harmony.

All the son of the sea asked in return for the protection he afforded the Manx folk, which enabled them to thrive, was a bundle of rushes. These would be brought to South Barrule on the eve of midsummer. Then the Islanders could walk away with light hearts, their rent paid for another year.[27]

When word came to Manannan that St Patrick was on his way, many years ago, the sea god cast his cloak over the Island; but Patrick found a way through the mist thanks to the birds and beasts, who innocently guided him to safety. He was not deceived by Manannan's ploy of making it seem like he was accompanied by a huge, spear wielding army. The Irishman chased the deity and his phantom fighters over the cliffs and across the sea to the enchanted isle. Manannan caused the island to sink beneath the waves and so escaped the wrath of St Patrick.[28]

Many people still bring rushes to Barrule at Midsummer, to honour him.

In January 2015, a statue of Manannan Mac Lir was stolen from Binevenagh Mountain in Northern Ireland. The area is known for its great natural beauty, incredible views and spectacular sunsets. A wooden cross bearing the words "You shall have no other Gods before me," was left in its stead.

A Manx friend mentioned the theft while we were chatting on the phone one afternoon, and I followed the story thereafter.

A Facebook post by PSNI (Police Service of Northern Ireland), Limavady, added a touch of humour to the situation. The reader of the "missing person" appeal could have been forgiven for thinking that "Manannan Mac" was a local sports star, though somewhat unconventionally dressed!

However, the appeal for the stolen sculpture – the work of talented Dungannon man, John Darren Sutton, who has also worked on the *Game of Thrones* series – had a sombre note too. The mention of Manannan's injured feet refers to the manner in which the statue was hacked from its prow-shaped plinth. In the opinion of its creator, this would have been a laborious procedure requiring the use of a power tool. Due to the statue's weight, the crime could not have been the work of one person.

A reward for the safe return of the sculpture – erected the previous year – was offered by a local businessman, who had a sentimental attachment to the site where the sea god overlooks Lough Foyle.

In the end, Manannan was discovered by ramblers just three hundred feet from his plinth. Yet, a search by air over the carpet of gorse and heather, at the time of his disappearance, revealed nothing. The group of walkers alerted soldiers who were there on a training exercise.

Manannan was in a sorry state. As well as damage to his feet, his head was beyond repair because he had fallen quite a distance. Local councillors agreed to replace the statue – an important part of the *Myths and Legends Trail*. Mr Sutton, once again, undertook the painstaking task. A year later, his second meticulous representation of the son of the sea was proudly standing in the remote location. Visitors flocked to welcome him home and to take photographs of, and be photographed with, the local celebrity! Reports of his theft and recovery had spread across the globe. Manannan even has his own Facebook page, though the posts, so plentiful at the time of his disappearance and replacement, have petered out.[29]

I was determined to pay homage to the returned hero too; but with one thing and another, the trip ended up on the long finger. Then, for a time, I feared that it wouldn't be possible at all.

One day, we will turn onto the Bishop's Road at Downhill and make the steep climb to where the road widens, and wild fuchsia bursts from the hedges on either side. He will be there on the hilltop, arms upraised – Manannan, keeper of secrets, custodian of hopes and dreams. They're safe with him.

I *will* make it to his side, however arduous it may be. Then my thoughts will turn to Mona, beloved of both our hearts.

***

During our final approach to Belfast City Airport, a man in the opposite aisle declared loudly that he thought we were about to land at an English airport in error! He couldn't see any familiar landmarks. Some of the other passengers began to panic.

A few said they thought the pilot had gone in the wrong direction when we took off from Ronaldsway! One lady was almost in tears because family members were waiting for her. They'd planned to go out for a meal, and a table had been booked. A few moments later, the man piped up again, saying this time that it was Belfast we were heading for! He'd just spotted Bombardier. Soaring blood pressure began to descend with the plane. Things look different in the dark. That man should not have spoken out as he did, alarming people unnecessarily. I was glad he got off the plane quite a bit ahead of me!

For many years, it seemed as if everything in my life took place in the dusk. I couldn't see things clearly because the acrid smoke of Summerland filled my mind, obscuring my thoughts. Charred memories were my constant companions. I believed that the future was something for other people to enjoy. Then I began to learn more about the tragic accident that changed my life. Knowledge brought understanding.

The smoke-blackened window I'd been gazing through since I was five years old, did not clear immediately; but gradually, little patches of light appeared, and I knew, although I couldn't see it yet, that the sun was shining brightly on the other side.

Chapter 4: Cobwebs at Christmas

During my trip to the Isle of Man in late 2016, I finally made it to Bar George. Although I'd often spoken of my intention to pay a visit, the opportunity hadn't presented itself until then. I left the Admiral House Hotel with clear instructions about how to get to the premises, situated on Hill Street, Douglas. The route seemed very straightforward. My decision to stay at the Admiral was based on the recommendation of a Manx friend, who felt it would be ideal because of its proximity to the town centre. The museum and library were within comfortable walking distance as Bar George should have been. Yet, more than an hour after I set off on my journey, with aching feet due to totally unsuitable footwear, I was still searching.

Close to the town hall – a building that was both familiar and comforting in my predicament – two ladies were walking along, deep in conversation. I apologised for interrupting them. The town was very quiet, and likely to remain that way, because of the time and the fact that it was a weeknight. There might not have been another opportunity. As we chatted, I realised that I'd passed the street I was looking for. I felt foolish, but the ladies were very kind. Armed with further directions, I set off again, reassured that I was only a few minutes away.

Some twenty minutes later, I began to think that Manannan was playing a trick on me by hiding Bar George from view. It seemed as if I was going to have to give in and return to Loch Promenade, to the warmth and comfort of my hotel room.

Leaning against a wall, to collect my thoughts and make a final decision, I looked up as I often do when I'm considering something. A cobweb dangling from a lamp post caught my eye. The delicate strands shimmered beneath the light. While thinking of the spider responsible for such painstaking work, I suddenly remembered a story from primary school!

A king who was fleeing from his enemies took refuge in a cave. The future seemed hopeless, and he was close to despair. Just then, his attention was captured by a little spider. It was trying to fix a silky strand to the damp wall. Time after time it failed in its task, but every time the spider fell it climbed the wall and tried again, until at last it succeeded. The determination shown by the little creature inspired the king. If a tiny spider refused to give up, then so would he. That king went on to win a very famous battle.

I have fallen many times in my life and have picked myself up and carried on. I would fall again two years after that November evening in Douglas, further and harder than I ever had before. It would take all my strength and determination to rise from the blow; but I would recall the spider who never gave up. I won't either.

I was angry with myself for giving a moment's thought to abandoning the search. Just as I was about to set off again, a man appeared on the opposite pavement. With renewed optimism, I called out. To my amazement, he crossed over and walked with me to the correct street, where the building I wanted was at the other end.

When I reached Bar George, I hesitated. The place I was about to enter had been a church hall before it became a bar and restaurant, and after the fire in Summerland it was a temporary morgue.

A few crisp leaves danced a little jig around my feet. The cool breeze that stirred them into a sudden flurry of activity stirred me too. I gripped the door handle firmly, and without further delay, took a deep breath and stepped into the past.

The purple glow inside reminded me of a restaurant I'd been to in the 1970s. It was an evening when I'd usually have been attending an organisation in our cold and draughty church hall. I had enjoyed the warmth, the ambience and slight feeling of unreality as much as the good food on that occasion.

Once settled at a table in Bar George, childhood memories came tiptoeing to the front of my mind.

Throughout childhood and as a young adult, the Bradbury Memorial Hall was a constant in my life. There were few weeks when I wasn't there at least once, unless it was holiday time. The period after the fire was an exception. When I finally returned I had changed, but the hall still looked the same.

Heaters placed high up on the walls were of little benefit unless you were standing directly underneath. The kitchen was coldest of all. There was a fusty smell, even in summer, particularly in the cupboards where the china tea set was stored. It had to be taken out and thoroughly washed before it could hold the steaming tea, plump sandwiches and home-baked cakes that would refresh parents and visitors after our annual "display" and prize-giving. Children had orange squash in paper cups, which was either anaemic or far too strong. We had our own fare too, though it was never as exciting as that reserved for the guests.

After our paper cups were empty and crumpled up, we looked for amusement while the adults ate and talked. The area under the stage held great fascination, but only the brave ventured there, as it was home to spiders and much larger, faster moving creatures! Grubby hands and knee socks told tales on those with enough courage to crawl in.

Although I thought the hall was old then, it was only in its third decade when we were pulling splinters from our palms, bare legs and woollen tights. We spent a lot of time playing games, often sitting cross-legged on the unvarnished wooden floor. The darning needle and tweezers would go to work on more stubborn skelfs later!

The atmosphere in the hall was different during Sunday school, there were no rambunctious games played then; but our Christmas party had an atmosphere that was quite unique.

For some reason, the Sunday school Christmas party took place in January. It was every bit as festive as parties that occurred during the previous month, perhaps more so because of the increased chance of snow. Santa Claus had delayed his return to the North Pole and was waiting in the back room of the hall. He would emerge while we were singing a festive song – that was his cue – carrying a sack of gifts over his shoulder. The smaller children stared at him wide-eyed, and even though their lips were moving no sound came out. Some of them had to be coaxed to approach the bearded figure to receive their present. I was a natural worrier and feared that my name wouldn't be called. It was not so much the loss of a gift that bothered me, but the shame of being forgotten. Thankfully, the dread I felt was unwarranted. There was always a parcel for Ruth. I was the only little girl with that name at the party.

My own children also attended Sunday school in the Bradbury hall. My father was "superintendent" by then. In the weeks before the Christmas party, I'd wrap the selection boxes which he would hand out dressed as Santa Claus. It was a task my eldest daughter took over, years later. She looks back with nostalgia on cosy afternoons at her grandparents' home, surrounded by rolls of brightly coloured paper and festive chocolate.

The Santa costume was an exceptional one, made for my sister's husband by his mother – a talented seamstress. Dad had taken their little boy to the event it was created for, and he had been bowled over by the suit's authenticity. My brother-in-law gave it to him afterwards, and Dad wore it proudly each year, enjoying the reaction he got. My sister found it in the attic of our family home after Dad died. It was passed on to his successor, so it would continue to make Christmas magical for the children of St Matthew's Sunday School, Broomhedge.

A new church hall was opened in 2001. My first visit was for Dad's funeral tea. Not even the ghost of our old hall remained, but in my dreams, like so many dear, familiar places from childhood, it's still the same.

***

As I looked around Bar George, at the beautiful dark wood counter and the tall shelves behind, I realised that if its history had been unfamiliar to me, I could not have guessed the building's previous purpose. Christmas menus stood on most of the tables, reminding me that I did possess that knowledge.

A photograph, posted by a Manx friend, on a social media site shows a group of nine youngsters dressed as angels, standing beneath a big, glittering star in St George's Church hall. Most of them have their arms crossed over their chests. I find the photo particularly poignant for several reasons.[30]

The children made their way to the front of the hall at the beginning of their nativity pageant, carefully carrying tall candle sticks in their small hands. Once the flickering pillars had been handed over, they gathered on the stage. The hard part was over. I'm sure parents and grandparents looked proudly at their little ones, dressed in pristine white, outwardly solemn as befitted their important role. Light glinted off halos perched above freshly brushed hair. It was the 1950s, and Derby Castle occupied the space where a "trail blazer"[31] would eventually stand. By the time an exciting new entertainment complex opened its doors to the public in their very own hometown, the children would be grown up. Some might even be parents themselves; but regardless of age, there would be something to suit everyone in Summerland and a very warm welcome for all.

I was just four years old when I took part in a Nativity play for the first time. I was an angel too, with sparkly wings. It seemed strange to be returning to school at night. We were ushered onto the stage and shuffled into position. Heavy curtains, that coughed dust, were tightly drawn in front of us. Beyond them, voices rose and fell. I wondered who the voices belonged to. There seemed to be so many of them! Nothing could have prepared me for the moment when the curtains groaned open, revealing a sea of faces. I was horrified. Although chatty with people I knew, I was shy with strangers, and there were hundreds in front of me and nowhere to hide.

Mum told me that she had never forgotten the frightened look on my face. Two glowing red spots replaced the rosy pink ones that people often remarked upon. I was wearing my new lilac dress – my favourite colour at the time – that Granny Jean had bought specially for the occasion. She was at home with baby Lynda. I'd waved cheerfully from the bottom of the path when she told me to enjoy my Nativity play, and Lynda waved her little hand back. I didn't know what Nativity meant, but because it was followed by the word play, I felt that it had to be something good.

I twisted handfuls of the lilac fabric nervously. Other children had spotted familiar faces in the audience. I scanned the rows frantically, and then I saw Mum. The seat next to her was empty.

Heavy traffic in the evenings meant delays, and Dad was often late home. His job as a sales representative took him all over the country, and he didn't have a "quitting" time like my friend's daddy. Even so, I began to fret. I was aware of the "Troubles" and feared that bad news would come knocking on our door. Just as the opening bars of the first carol were being played, there was a noise at the back of the room. The double doors clicked shut, and a man made his way towards the row where Mum was sitting, then carefully across to the empty chair beside her, mindful of handbags and toes as he went. The butterflies in my tummy ceased their furious flapping. Everything would be ok now because my daddy had arrived. Nothing bad could happen when he was there!

At the end of the concert, when everyone was beginning to leave, I heard one of the adults call to a teacher, "That's it over for another year!" I felt so happy. A year was a long, long time. There would be a lot of water under the bridge, as Gran would have said, before I needed to think about the Nativity play again. Little did I know, that appearing on stage in my primary school would be the least of my worries the following December. In fact, it wouldn't be on my mind at all! The lilac dress, washed and ironed, would be stored away with other things I'd grown out of, for Lynda to wear when the time came. She would wear them even if they weren't her favourite colour because that's the way it was. There would be no new dress for me that Christmas. The angel wings I had worn when I was four, would be worn by another child. They'd have lost some of their glitter by then, but only some. *All* the shine would be gone from my short life.

When a much-diminished Summerland was preparing to welcome the public again, a new generation filled St George's Hall. The first floor of the big building rang with innocent laughter. Young Manx boys and girls were having a wonderful time at their Christmas party. A table close to the door was laden with paper bags containing an orange and sweets. These would be given out when all the games had been played, and it was time to go home. Those at the back of the queue might watch the dwindling pile anxiously, but no one would be disappointed; there was a bag for each child present.

It's unlikely that any of the youngsters, who clattered down the stairs and into the cool December air, to begin their journey home, knew of the sad period in the hall's history. There would be time enough to learn the awful truth. The bright flame of childhood burns such a short while, but the memories made then last a lifetime. Let them be good ones.

When I was a young mum, I witnessed an elderly lady rebuking another parent for smacking her children. "Don't beat them," she said. "Life will beat them enough."

I tugged my mind back to the present. Keen to discover more about my surroundings: the building's transformation from sacred to secular, I had asked a member of staff if there was anyone who could help. He brought me a little card with some contact details on it.

When I tucked the card into my bag, which was stuffed with notebooks, a novel, ring binder and sundry items, I nicked the tip of my finger on a sharp edge. It throbbed, as cuts of that nature always do. A few drops of blood fell onto the floor, while I scrabbled for a tissue. As I bent down to dab them up, the past caught me unawares. It still had much to say.

Dudley Butt was a detective with the CID in 1973. In his capacity as a Scenes of Crime Officer, Dudley went to Summerland on the morning of 3rd August, to investigate the cause of the fire. Later, the local force was joined by forensic experts who had travelled to the Isle of Man from Lancashire. The first floor of St George's Hall became their headquarters. As well as taking photos and being involved in the post-mortems, Dudley was in contact with bereaved relatives. That must have been a very difficult task.[32]

An extensive search led police to Liverpool, eleven days after the fire. Five weeks later, at a juvenile court hearing in Douglas, three schoolboys pleaded guilty when charged with damaging a lock on the kiosk at Summerland. The value of the lock was one pound. Each boy was fined three pounds, on top of which were costs of fifteen pence and compensation of thirty-three pence.[33]

I've always been curious about where the Liverpool boys were staying at the time of the fire. A while ago, I found out that it may have been a property on the Strathallan Road, known locally as the Colby Cubbin Home. The late Mr Cubbin was a local benefactor.

A driver employed by Douglas Corporation Transport in the 1960s, remembers collecting groups of children who had just arrived on the boat. He would take them to the big house, where they were warmly greeted by the couple who ran the establishment. Refreshments were waiting for the excited youngsters, thirsty after their journey; and there was plenty of cake and a pot of tea for the driver too![34]

A wonderful holiday on the beautiful Isle of Man, with good food and lots to do and see, was enjoyed by many children who travelled from the adjacent isle to stay in the lovely cliff-top property.

I've also read that the cliff house provided holiday accommodation for Liverpool residents, of all ages, throughout the year.

When I last made enquiries, some years ago, I was told that the beautiful nineteenth century house, described as "A Gentleman's Residence," was up for sale.[35]

It may have been the case that some of the children, who stayed there over the years, did not have the same opportunities as others, and perhaps their young lives were troubled in some way. I was interested to read that Dudley Butt was also "Champion for children and young people in care."[36]

I recently discovered that one of the Liverpool boys came to the Island with his parents, the day before the fire. Now I am left wondering how the three of them got to know each other in such a short time. Did they meet in Summerland on 1st August, or did their paths cross elsewhere during the countdown to tragedy? Maybe they only became acquainted at Summerland on the evening of the fire. Young people make friends very quickly. Is it possible that one, or all, of them had been to the complex on a previous holiday?

I have spent many hours deliberating the actions of the boys: considering whether they had a fascination with fire, the way some people do. They admitted to their counsel that ignition was caused by a match, not a cigarette as they had previously claimed.[37] Was breaking the lock on the kiosk and what followed next, just something to do on a damp evening?

The boys ran away from the burning kiosk. I read an account, that appeared in a paper, a few days after the fire. The man interviewed – a thirty-year-old PE teacher, from Winsford – who alerted a member of staff to the blaze, said that he saw two boys "laughing and joking" as they fled the scene. Although, he could have caught hold of them, he felt it imperative to raise the alarm and indeed, the rapid spread of fire to the outer wall of Summerland bore this out.[38] I remember situations during my teenage years, when my friends and I laughed at the least appropriate times. We just couldn't stop, even when we were told off. It was nervous laughter.

I've given a lot of thought to the different associations we have with fire; and of what it meant to me in the innocent days before Summerland and of how I've viewed it since.

During my childhood, many of our relatives and family friends lived in rural areas. Not everyone we visited had a television set. Some who did possess one only switched it on to watch the news or a particular programme. For a few it was an object of awe, others eyed it with suspicion. One lady combed her hair and took off her apron, for fear that those inside the "box" could see her. I definitely believed this to be the case and regularly held objects of interest to the screen. Though my belief gradually waned when Miss Helen failed to spot me in her magic mirror, time after time! The television was never on when there were guests. An elderly relation, we called on regularly, had an ornament on top of her TV, which proclaimed that it was a souvenir from the Isle of Man! It was a place that had no meaning for me then. In the absence of something to occupy me, while the adults chatted, I'd gaze into the hearth looking for shapes in the flames and soon succumbed to the hypnotic effect. Mum gently woke me when it was time to go. Baby Lynda had been roused from her slumber too. She expressed her displeasure when cold air nipped her plump cheeks as the swollen front door creaked open. My pleasant dreams drifted away to mingle with the smoke that puffed gently from the chimney of the little ivy-covered house. Fire was my friend then.

In the years after Summerland, I often stayed with Granny Jean – Mum's mother. (We were very close and became even more so because of what happened. She travelled to the Island with one of my paternal uncles, to support us. When I woke up crying in hospital, she was by my side.)

There was always a delicious smell in Granny's kitchen. When she opened the door of the range to poke the glowing coals, which made the saucepans bubble, I shivered a little despite the heat, and I was glad when she closed it again. When the sitting room fire threatened to go out, I no longer volunteered to breathe life into it with the bellows – a task I had previously enjoyed.

When Grandad lit an autumn bonfire, to dispose of nature's debris, I turned away from the flames, terrified of the images I might see there.

I was aware that fire could, not only, destroy things we no longer want but people and lives too! It had to be carefully managed.

A few elderly relations still cooked on an open fire in those post-Summerland days. My maternal great-grandmother suffered a stroke while cooking her lunch. She fell on the floor next to the hearth, but it could have been so much worse. I had watched the process many times, during which she would stoop over the pot to test the potatoes with a fork, and the thought of a different outcome haunted me. Granny Liza was in her nineties then, and although her days of cooking "spuds" were over, she lived until she was one hundred and six and added a second "great" to her title when my first child was born.

I had no dealings with the coal fire in our family home, though I knew Mum and Dad were more than cautious. It was removed when circumstances permitted, and an electric fire was installed instead.

When I was an adult, although I hated the open fire in my new home – the only form of heating – I was in control. I stayed up until I was certain it had gone out.

I worried that the people in charge of any building I went into wouldn't realise how dangerous fire can be: how it can begin as a tiny spark and rapidly grow to monstrous proportions; barring the way of those trying to flee from it.

I've wondered if the three boys lit a fire because they were angry about something or with someone. In my own angry phase, I made the point that not all people who have had bad things happen to them or who have been let down in some way, will commit an offence. I suffered greatly in the years after the tragedy, but I never felt the need to damage someone else's property or endanger life; but I hadn't taken into consideration things that are done without forethought. In December 2018, I remembered a foolish act when I was a similar age to one of the Liverpool boys. It was something I did on the spur of the moment, without thinking of the consequences.

During the last weeks of 2018, I had plenty of time to think, confined as I was to a hospital bed. Christmas was approaching, and I longed to be in the real world, far away from the clinical environment that had become my home. The window in my small room was too high up to show anything other than a patch of sky. I could hear the birds singing, and although I couldn't see them it helped to know they were there.

Nystagmus and double vision prevented me from reading, and I had to listen to, rather than watch, the television on the wall. My caregivers gave cheery accounts of the festive preparations they were making, of parties they had been to and meals they had eaten. My nourishment was supplied by a nasal tube. I smiled and tried hard to be happy for them, but I was crying inside. I didn't know what would become of me in the weeks and months ahead.

Nights were hardest of all. Sleep evaded me. I was alone and in pain; the kind of pain no drug could relieve. The only comfort I had, in those long, lonely hours, was the memory of my old life: the life that had been so cruelly snatched away, just when I had begun to feel positive about the future. As I lay in the dark, after one particularly tough day, I thought of how Christmas had been, for me and my family, in the past. I began to recall each one as far back as I could remember.

Santa brought me a red tricycle in 1969. I could only move it along with my toes in the beginning, but by the summer I was able to pedal it up and down the garden path. My strong young limbs carried out the task with ease.

In December 1973, at the age of five, I was learning to walk again, and although my skin grafts were stiff and painful, with physiotherapy my mobility would improve. I did not have that guarantee four and a half decades on.

When a church clock, in the distance, chimed three times, I had reached my teenage years, and that is when it appeared: the memory so carefully stored away at the back of my mind. Perhaps my vulnerability brought it to the fore. I had let my guard down.

More, much more than Christmas Day, I relished the run up to the great event. Everyone seemed happy and greeted one another cheerfully. (As I grew older, I realised that wasn't always the case. People fell ill and lost their lives at Christmas too. For us, the season is now tinged with sadness, but we treasure the happy memories.) School was winding down for the holidays, and we were practicing for concerts and carol services. We were also making things to take home at the end of term.

I loved making things, and Christmas was the perfect time to be creative. To my great delight one evening at Girls Brigade, we were told to bring what was needed to make a Yule log the following week. I was looking forward to it even more than the carol singing, which I thoroughly enjoyed. This involved a walk along the Kesh Road, almost as far as the famous Down Royal Racecourse. Our breath made "smoke" in the frosty air when we sang for the smiling residents of the houses we called at. No one minded that heat was escaping while they stood on their doorsteps, relishing the tradition as much as we did. Hot soup was waiting when we returned to the church hall, with noses to rival Rudolph's, another step closer to Christmas!

Our local shop had a small supply of festive novelties on a shelf behind the till. I spied a pack of candles which I immediately fell in love with. On either side of a miniature Christmas tree, stood a little wax snowman and a jolly Santa Claus. I reckoned the snowman would be a perfect centrepiece for my log.

Everything went without a hitch. I was bursting with pride when I rushed home to show off my wonderful creation! It sat on the right side of the hearth looking pretty.

A few days later, I studied it carefully and thought how nice it would be to have a matching log for the other side. I didn't have another snowman candle, but Santa Claus was lovely as well, and I had plenty of other supplies left over. In my bedroom, I busily fixed an abundance of cotton wool to the wooden surface with enough glue to ensure that it would never come off!

Working on the project alone, without the friendly chatter of the other girls and the encouragement of the leaders, wasn't as enjoyable, but I carried on. Soon my log was twinkling to rival the stars. Mum would have something to say about the glitter all over the carpet and the considerable quantity stuck to my clothes; but those details could be addressed later! I carried my new work of art downstairs, keen to discover if it would have the desired effect. It did! If only I had been content to leave it at that…

Suddenly, I was overcome by a strong desire to see how the Yule logs would look with the candles lit. It wasn't my intention to destroy the lovely little wax figures, but I thought that a second or two wouldn't do any damage. Surely, they wouldn't melt!

My parents were chatting in the kitchen, while they did the dishes together. On the mantelpiece, behind an ornament, sat a box of matches. Plate chinked against plate; the hum of conversation continued behind the closed door. I turned off the light, then reached for the matches and quickly struck one. A flame flickered on top of Santa's hat, where the wick emerged, before growing taller. Then, to my absolute horror, the cotton wool ignited! Although the kitchen was only a few feet away, I panicked. As well as being in trouble for my foolish, reckless actions, I knew the sight of the flames would upset my parents and bring back terrible memories. I rushed for the stairs, causing the flames to grow higher. If only I could get to the bathroom! But I couldn't hold the log any longer, it was burning my hands! It fell onto the step above and rolled to the bottom, which mercifully extinguished the flames.

I was shaking from head to foot, and my heart was pounding. I stayed in my room for the rest of the evening. When I was certain that everyone was asleep, I took the log, now in a sorry state – both charred and soggy from the soaking I gave it – downstairs and put it at the bottom of the outside bin and the incident to the back of my mind; eventually. There were frequent dreams of being trapped on a burning staircase, before that happened.

***

I was keen for Christmas to make an appearance in my own home, when I returned from the Isle of Man. There was still a lot of work ahead in terms of finishing *Made in Summerland*; it was a daunting thought. Rooting out the decorations would be a welcome diversion. Though, what I really needed was reassurance that it would all come together in the end. The artificial tree, cocooned in black refuse sacks, reposed in a distant corner of the shed. A real one wasn't an option because of my wheezy chest. Some of the longer branches had poked holes through the plastic, and dangling from one of them, next to a stubborn piece of tinsel, was a little cobweb…

Chapter 5: Somewhere Around the Corner

"As they set forth, encircling their loved homeland
On eager wing; then heading out to sea,
Were borne away upon their last long journey;
Swept from our sight – but not from memory."

(*In Memoriam*, by Kathleen Faragher)[39]

In December 2016, I developed carpal tunnel syndrome, made worse by the cold. Our central heating had broken down, and I felt a little like Bob Cratchit, who, bent over a candle stub scratched away at his desk, a few dying embers in the grate his only cheer.[40]

Christmas at Tullycarn took place without fuss. Soon, it was as far away as ever.

New Year's Eve brought with it the ninth anniversary of Dad's passing. We didn't celebrate the end of the old year and the arrival of the new. We never had, even when Dad was well. It seems a melancholy time, and I prefer to let Janus reminisce about the twelve months gone by and ponder what the next twelve have in store.

Winter wearied eventually, and there were little hints that spring was close at hand.

The penultimate day of February marked fifty-nine years since the Winter Hill air disaster. A Manx friend shared the heart-breaking story with me some years ago, and I was moved to tears. When snowdrops push through the hardened earth, with strength contrary to their fragile appearance, I think of the men who perished on the lonely hillside; its name so apt that dreadful day and of their loved ones, left behind.

Another air disaster, that occurred at the beginning of the same month in 1958, is much talked of and widely remembered compared to the Manx tragedy, in which more lives were lost.

Thirty-nine men, the majority of whom were connected, in some way, with the Isle of Man's motor trade, gathered in the cosy departure lounge of Ronaldsway Airport. All were in great form. Despite the frosty morning, winter was almost over. They were free from work and heading off on a trip to *Exide* in Manchester: an excursion arranged by Ramsey Motors. After visiting the battery factory, the men were to attend a motor show before flying home to their families. The day, however, would not pan out as intended. All the careful plans were about to be torn asunder.

In the Lancashire towns of Bolton and Horwich, there was no evidence that spring was elbowing winter out of its way. Earlier in the week, an unexpected blizzard brought daily life almost to a standstill. It was the worst weather the area had seen for nearly twenty years.

Around seven miles from Bolton and just under five from Horwich, lies Winter Hill. The location is desolate and brooding during the darker months, but when spring breezes blow the shadows away it becomes transformed. A spectacular view, from the peak, rewards the walker when the weather is fair. On such a day, the heart is light and the soul joyful; but when that golden orb, which lifts the spirits, is hidden from sight, the mood on the moor quickly changes. Local legend claims that only ill-luck can be expected when the hill dons a cap of mist. The past clambers from the gloom then, with fetid breath, hissing ugly secrets, tapping bone upon earth encrusted bone, centuries old.

Despite the freezing weather, the Independent Television Authority (ITA) transmitting station, on the summit of Winter Hill, was warm and cosy inside. Close to it stood a mast, four hundred and forty-five feet tall; both were only a few years old in 1958. The mast was best avoided in freezing weather because of the risk of falling ice. On that fateful February Thursday, building and mast were nestled in deep snow and cloaked in dense fog. It must have seemed to the engineers on duty as if they were the only people on earth. Every eventuality had been catered for, due to the building's remote location. There was even a stretcher, should the worst happen. Although, the hope was that it would never be needed.

The vehicle that usually brought the engineers to work, couldn't make it the last few miles on the morning of 27th, because of drifted snow, and the men on the rota that day had to walk. When they finally arrived at the station, shaking snow from their clothes, they had no idea that disaster would shortly come knocking on the door.

***

During his years of employment in the tyre and battery industry, my father went on many trips like the one that ended in tragedy for thirty-five men from the Isle of Man. He would wake us early on the morning of his departure, to say goodbye; that was important to him. It was too soon for me to get up, but sleep had flown. I'd worry from the moment he left until I heard his key turning in the lock again. I knew he would bring us presents, always choosing well and delighting his little girls with his generosity and thoughtfulness, but I couldn't think of gifts when he was so far away. All I wanted was my daddy home, safe and well. Our family was incomplete in his absence. Life didn't feel right.

Jack Cretney, a police sergeant in the force's motor patrol, was one of the passengers on the chartered flight to Manchester. The father of two young boys had been invited on the day trip because Ramsey Motors supplied the car driven by the patrol. Jack, whose amiable disposition made him popular with colleagues, finished his nightshift a few hours before dawn. He was ready and waiting when his lift to the airport arrived. The eldest Cretney boy Alan, waved his dad off; a moment that he has never forgotten.

By lunchtime, news of the dreadful plight of the Bristol Wayfarer and its passengers had made it to the Cretney home. It arrived just before the boys returned from school for their midday meal. It was known that there were some survivors, but their identity had not yet been established.

Alan and his younger brother listened to updates on the wireless. The Cretney family didn't have a telephone, and the boys had to walk to a public phone box, at regular intervals, to call a special number. With the passing of the hours, it seemed increasingly unlikely that the news would be positive. Next day, official confirmation came: the boys would never see their daddy again. Mrs Cretney dedicated her life to her sons and raised fine men.

Both Alan and David followed in their late father's footsteps, by choosing a career in the police force – David, after a spell in the Merchant Navy. Jack would have been so proud! His grandsons serve in the Isle of Man Constabulary too.

Alan was given his late father's watch, which stopped at the time of the crash. It was a hard thing for a youngster to come to terms with – a beloved daddy leaving home at breakfast time and only his personal effects coming back.

It snowed on the day Jack Cretney was buried with the honour of a police funeral. It snowed when they put my father in the cold earth too.

I was thirty-nine when I said goodbye to my dad, for the last time, and as unprepared to lose him then as I would have been when I was a little girl. I feel fortunate to have had him in my life for so long, and I cherish the memories of special moments he shared with us. It took a long time for the world to make sense again after Dad's death, and I still miss him very much. We need our parents, no matter what age we are.

Alan's recollections of 27th February 1958 are as vivid now as they were on that awful day – just as my memories of Summerland are, which some people find surprising.

Howard Callow was only four years old when disaster changed his life. There are no fuzzy edges for him either.

Winter Hill was a subject Howard avoided for a long time, though his memories never dimmed. For more than four and a half decades, he couldn't bring himself to visit the scene of the dreadful crash in which his father Thomas perished; but after reading a book about the tragedy, he felt the need to see the site for himself. Supported by his son and accompanied by the president of Horwich Rotary Club, Howard laid a wreath where the doomed plane, victim of a navigational error, spilled its precious cargo into the snow, leaving twenty-seven widows and thirty-three children without their father. Most of the children were less than ten years old. One was a new baby.

A minor illness meant no school for young Howard on the day his daddy left for Manchester. While he was snuggled up in bed, the BBC news came on the wireless. Howard called for his mum. The reporter was speaking about a plane crash. Mrs Callow had a bad feeling, and unfortunately, her gut instinct was correct. She was now a widow with two small children to bring up. Since Howard first joined Horwich Rotary Club's annual walk to the spot where the Wayfarer, owned by Silver Cities Airways, lay broken, twenty feet short of the hill's summit and a matter of minutes away from its destination, two significant anniversaries have taken place.

Some of the men who died in the air disaster were members of Douglas Rotary Club, and several of those who helped with the rescue operation belonged to Horwich Rotary Club, including the station engineer Bill Jarvis, who was first at the dreadful scene. He later received a prestigious award.

Speaking ahead of the sixtieth anniversary, Rotarian Howard Callow explained about the enduring friendship between the two clubs. Regular visits to the Isle of Man by members of Horwich Rotary Club and vice versa, mean that members of both clubs are completely familiar with each other's towns and lives.

Howard travelled to the adjacent isle with around twenty-four others in February 2018, to attend a service near the crash site. There was an exhibition at Horwich Heritage Centre, to mark the significant anniversary. Footage of the aftermath of the disaster and films of commemorative events in 2008, were shown then too.

On the Isle of Man, a service took place in Cooil y Ree Park, St John's, before the Winter Hill memorial plaque, which had been put in place by Douglas Rotary Club on the fiftieth anniversary. (A tree was planted at the same time.) The inscription on the plaque, as well as remembering the lives lost, pays tribute to Horwich Rotary Club for the help they gave and for a long friendship born out of tragedy.

The Island's lieutenant governor was also in attendance at the event in 2018, during which music was provided by the Ellan Vannin Pipe Band and Douglas Town Band. In typically generous Manx spirit, the proprietor of a local café opened its doors to those attending the service. Refreshments in the warmth and comfort of Green's were greatly appreciated.

Ten days after the fatal plane crash in Lancashire, a service had been held in St George's Church, Douglas, in memory of the victims. A lesson was read to the packed congregation by lieutenant governor, Sir Ambrose Flux Dundas, who had been in office since 1952. He was succeeded the following year. Sir Ambrose passed away in 1973, a few months before the Summerland fire.

[On the fiftieth anniversary of the tragedy, a memorial plaque was placed on a gate post close to where thirty-four of the men from the Isle of Man died. (Another man passed away in hospital.) The plaque is the joint effort of Douglas and Horwich Rotary Clubs.]

Susan, who was seven when her father died in the air disaster, didn't begin to grieve properly until she was a mother herself. The enormity of her loss really struck her then. The subject was too distressing for her mother to talk about, which left many questions unanswered.

In the beginning, Susan and her siblings were shielded from the awful truth, then their mother had the heart-breaking task of explaining that daddy had gone away forever. Like many of the crash's widows, the young woman devoted her life to raising her children.

Loving relations did all they could to protect the youngsters bereaved by the tragedy on Winter Hill, but there were some blows they couldn't cushion. They couldn't prevent cruel remarks being made by other children. Those hurt more than anything. I know that from experience.

Arthur Gleave's daughter remembers the smell of her dad's workplace clearly. I know exactly the smell she means. Her daddy worked with batteries, just like mine had, and Exide is a name I remember well. Smells evoke so many memories….

When I open the door of my husband's workshop, I'm transported to my grandad's garage at a time before the fire in Summerland. I would amuse myself while he was occupied with his latest project; content just to be near him. I loved the smell of petrol, oil and grease. If Grandad got some on his hands he wiped them on a rag, not on his overalls. It wasn't as easy to do the laundry then, and he was a thoughtful man. As a reward for my patience, Grandad poured some water into a pool of oil, enjoying my reaction when I stirred it with a stick. The result never failed to amaze me! During the worst days of my life, when everything seemed to be the colour of despair, I thought about the magic in the puddle. All I needed was a sprinkle of hope to create a beautiful rainbow, with a world full of happiness on the other side.

For Olga Gray, the smell of dust, a steaming kettle or a freshly washed bone china cup triggered memories of a very sad time in her life.

A solemn procession made its way to a church hall in Horwich. Kind faces greeted the visitors. Cups of tea were placed into cold hands. It was difficult for anyone to find the right thing to say in the circumstances. The room began to fill with steam as more water was boiled for further cups of tea. It was something to do, when the right words wouldn't come.

One by one, the visitors left the hall for the building next door, where a distressing task awaited them.

Many people have told me that they'd planned to visit Summerland on the night of the fire, and then decided to go somewhere else instead. Often the change of plan was a last minute one.

The proprietor of the Empire Garage, in Peel, decided that the trip to the Exide factory was just too much, as he was in the middle of a house move. A coin was tossed to determine which of his employees would take his place. Selwyn Lace won. He would be travelling to Manchester, with thirty-eight other men from the Isle of Man, on the day before his thirty-eighth birthday!

Speaking on Manx Radio, prior to the fiftieth anniversary of the "worst air disaster in the Island's history," Selwyn's younger sister, Olga Gray, spoke of his zeal for all things motorbike related! She fondly remembered the lane at the back of their childhood home as always being full of dismantled bikes; and recalled that Selwyn spent much of his youth at the Salisbury Garage, in Douglas. Teddy Christian, the manager, also lost his life on Winter Hill.

Billy and David Harding had gone on the Manchester trip to represent their family motorcycle business. Billy was well known for his prowess in riding his scrambler (Motocross bike) on the Island's popular courses. Gilbert Harding received the dreadful news that his sons were among the fatalities.

Olga was a young married woman, living in Liverpool, when news about the fallen flight reached her. A night of uncertainty followed the distressing phone call from her sister. Selwyn's name wasn't on the list of deceased, nor did it appear in a local paper with all the others. This was because he'd been using his employer's ticket. Security wasn't as tight then, and there had been no need to change the details. By dawn, sad reality had settled in the hearts of Selwyn's family, who were already under pressure because of their mother's illness. All hope was gone.

Friends and relatives of the deceased boarded the steamer the day after the crash. Black cars awaited the arrival of the Isle of Man boat. Olga was waiting at the docks too. She was going to Horwich for the same reason as the others. It was the last thing she could do for Selwyn. Olga was just twenty-two years old, when she was asked to confirm the identity of her dear big brother in the Methodist church, which had become a temporary mortuary following the plane crash.

Selwyn Lace's sister and brother-in-law had been surprised to discover there was nothing to commemorate the lives lost, when they visited the television transmitting station, some twenty-one years after the tragedy. (Olga hadn't felt able to return before then.) They were keen to change the situation.

In Summerland, those who decided to remain on the Solarium floor, rather than climb to the upper terraces, had unwittingly given themselves the best chance of escaping when fire broke out.

Norman Ennett wasn't sitting in the cabin, with the stewardess and the rest of the passengers, when the Wayfarer, operated by Manx Airlines on the fateful trip to Manchester, struck Winter Hill during its final approach to Ringway Airport. Norman, who knew the plane's captain well, had been invited to sit in the cockpit. His decision to accept the offer, coupled with the way in which the aircraft was designed, most likely saved his life. Although *Charlie Sierra* cartwheeled on impact, and the captain sustained life changing injuries, the three occupants of the cockpit (above the substantial nose cone) survived.

Stewardess, Jennifer Curtis (Jennifer Fleet upon her marriage), had been sitting in the tail section of the plane filling in paperwork. Seated close to her was Harold Williamson. Both were thrown through the air and landed in the snow, but they managed to struggle back to their seats where they waited for help. This arrived in the form of the co-pilot Bill Howarth, who'd grabbed the first aid box and come to do what he could, before setting off to raise the alarm.

Bill somehow managed to make his way through the mist and snow, three hundred and fifty yards, to the remote transmitting station. If he had gone the other direction help may not have come until it was too late, and he too would likely have perished as the route was even more perilous. What a shock for the engineers on duty there: a man in a pilot's uniform, bleeding from injuries and in a distressed state, appearing suddenly as if from nowhere! Telephone calls were made from the station to summon emergency services, but they would find it very difficult to access the crash site. Engineers left immediately, with their hearts in their mouths, prepared for an arduous trek, knowing that catastrophe awaited them.

Mr Williamson, who worked for the Isle of Man Electricity Board, recalled that two other passengers, who had been sitting in the seats behind him at the beginning of the journey, decided to move further forward during the flight. Those men did not survive when the cabin disintegrated. I have never changed seat on a plane since learning of the fate of the Bristol Wayfarer.

After a week in hospital with broken bones, lacerations and a head injury so alarming that his wife didn't recognise him, Norman Ennett was flown home. It was three months before he was fit for work again. Norman recalls his father going to one funeral after the other, and he has never forgotten the devastating effect the disaster had on the Island's garage industry. Norman's father had been invited to go on the trip as they sold Exide batteries, but the older man didn't like flying, so his son went instead.

We can try to ignore the past, or put it behind us, but it is always ready to catch us unawares.

Spain was home to Norman Ennett, during the winter months, for several years; and that is where the past tapped him on the shoulder when he least expected it. While in a bar one evening, he started to chat to a man who turned out to be from Bolton! Winter

Hill was mentioned in the conversation, and Norman explained about being caught up in the 1958 disaster. He made the surprising discovery that his new companion had played a part too! A doctor had made his way to the crash site on foot, because the roads were impassable. He was accompanied by another man, who had carried his bag. His assistant that day was a gentleman whose chemist shop was in Horwich. Many miles from both their homes and several decades later, Norman found himself face to face with that very man! What a small world it is!

Although Norman visited Bolton on a number of occasions, he had no urge to see the disaster site again. He attended the event at St John's, to mark the passing of fifty years, but it wasn't until the sixtieth anniversary was approaching that he felt able to return to the moor. Norman was eighty-four years old, and the last remaining survivor of the tragedy, when he finally made the journey. Snow lay on the hill that day, too, making the commemoration all the more poignant.

It would be forty-two years before Manx police sergeant, Bill Brown, visited the spot where his father Norman died. The Manchester trip had great appeal for Norman, not only because of his line of business, but also due to the location of the Exide Factory. He had been looking forward to it so much.

It was summer when Bill stood with his son, daughter and police officers from the local area, while an aviation historian explained how the Biffer (the tragic Wayfarer's nickname), and its passengers, met with disaster.

On the day of the crash, Bill, recovering from an operation, was manning the desk in Douglas Police Station. He had already taken a disturbing call from his mother concerning his father's dog. The spaniel had been behaving totally out of character, clearly upset by something even though their home was remote. An hour later, Bill answered the call that brought devastating news to the Manx community.

Bill knew nearly everyone who died, and he was able to identify many of them, relieving the burden for their relatives, despite his own grief. His help in the aftermath of the disaster was invaluable. Bill returned to Mona's Isle on the chartered plane that brought the thirty-five deceased Manxmen back to the Isle of Man, and their devastated families. He was on duty again that night; such were the times.

Memories of the day his grandfather died have not faded for John Brown. He was taken out of school when the awful news came, and spent the afternoon and evening with his dad Bill, who had the unenviable task of visiting homes where fathers, sons and brothers left that morning, in such high spirits, oblivious of the horror ahead.

Only a year after John and his sister went to Winter Hill with their dad, they said a final goodbye to him.

Norman Brown was seventy when he boarded the Bristol Wayfarer with his friends, believing that he was just a short journey away from a dream coming true. A farm previously stood where the Exide factory was constructed; a farm where Norman had been raised.

Mr Fred Kennish, who sadly passed away in 2011, was also on the ill-fated flight.

Once they were told it was safe to do so, Fred loosened his seatbelt slightly as did Jimmy Crosbie, his friend and partner in the business of Crosbie, Cain and Kennish – coach builders. They might have been more comfortable without the belts, dressed as they were in suits and heavy overcoats; but the fact that they didn't unfasten them may have saved their lives.

Fred remembered flying over Blackpool and being able to see the damage that fire had done to the pier, just ten days before. Next time he looked through the plane window, mist had obscured everything. After that, there was nothing. When he recovered consciousness in Bolton Royal Infirmary, about a week later, Jimmy Crosbie was in the next bed.

Although, he hadn't any memories of the actual crash, Fred recalled struggling to breathe, while crying out for his wife, at some point afterwards. This was due to a punctured lung, which made it seem that any air he managed to take in was going straight out of his back – a terrifying experience.

The two Manxmen didn't know anyone in their ward, and they clung to the slim hope that their friends were in another part of the hospital. A few weeks would pass before they learnt the dreadful truth, that including themselves, only four of the passengers had made it.

Soon, Fred was the sole crash survivor left in the Bolton hospital. The plane's captain had been transferred to a different hospital and the other survivors allowed home. It was a distressing time for him, and he felt very alone.

By the time Fred was discharged, two months later, thirty-five funerals had taken place. The entire Island was affected by the tragedy – referred to as "Black Thursday," by the Speaker of the House of Keys.

On the day Fred returned to the Isle of Man – an emotional home-coming because so many of his friends were gone – a complication occurred with his badly injured leg. He was taken to hospital, where he received the stark news that the leg would have to be amputated. This was to take place at Broadgreen, in Liverpool; but fortune was smiling on Fred Kennish.

When rescuers came across him on Winter Hill, the Manxman's leg was lying across his chest, barely connected to his body. It had been encased in plaster during his time in Bolton, to see if the damaged bone would knit. At the Liverpool hospital, a wonderful surgeon performed a delicate operation, removing splinters of bone without puncturing a major vessel. Six long months of traction followed the procedure. Although many outpatient visits would be necessary, and Fred would continue to experience pain from the injury throughout his life, he kept his leg. The operation was a success.

It was nothing short of miraculous that Fred survived the crash which robbed him of so many friends. His body had been in a shocking state, and the men who were first at the scene of utter devastation believed him to be beyond help. After straightening him up and folding his arms across his chest, they moved on to other passengers whose condition looked more hopeful. Broken shoulder blades and collar bones, caused by his suit jacket and overcoat being torn off on impact, were just a few of Fred's extensive injuries. Wearing only vest and trousers, he lay in the snow.

After the engineers carried the other survivors to the warmth of the station – an extremely tough journey for both rescuers and injured over uneven ground, where dips and hollows were concealed by snow – they returned for Fred, but there was no sign of him.

When Fred Kennish was elected to the position of Mayor of Douglas in 1989, it gave him the opportunity to achieve something that had been on his mind since 1958. Funds were raised for a plaque to commemorate the thirty-five Islanders; and to acknowledge the tremendous aid given by the residents of Bolton and Horwich. Survivors and relatives of the deceased travelled, courtesy of Manx Airlines, to see the memorial stone being unveiled.

The words on the plaque, that Horwich Rotary Club arranged to be erected on the wall of the transmitting station, express how Fred felt about all those who were a shining light in a dark time.

Michael Gray remembered the day of the unveiling as being in complete contrast to the one that claimed the life of his brother-in-law, Selwyn. It was a bright, sunny day with lark song overhead.

A visit to the crash site followed the ceremony, which was also attended by the mayors of Bolton and Horwich. A past attempt by Fred to grow daffodils, in tribute to his lost friends, proved futile. The ground was still saturated with aviation fuel; even grass struggled to grow there. The scarred earth is a permanent reminder of the tragedy.

Bits of wood and metal lay in a shallow grave, undisturbed, until fumbling fingers extracted fragments; sad souvenirs were slipped into suit pockets. It was a small measure of comfort; a way to keep lost loved ones close.

During a visit to Horwich Fire Station, to express their gratitude, Mr and Mrs Kennish were chatting about the accident to two of the men there, when realisation dawned. Fred was almost overcome by emotion by what he heard. Quite incredibly, he had finally met one of his lifesavers in the flesh. The retired fireman explained that he and a colleague had been carrying bodies to the transmitting station. At first glance, it seemed as if the Manxman, who was lying in a drift of snow, had also passed away. Then the fireman became aware that he was still alive. Using their belts, the men strapped Fred to a ladder and began the difficult descent.

The Douglas Mayor and Mayoress also visited the hospital where Fred had been looked after so well.

When word of the plane crash arrived at Bolton Royal Infirmary, wheels were set in motion and preparations made to receive a great number of casualties. Rather than be dismayed at the prospect of longer shifts and an increased workload, staff were relieved that so many must have survived; but the reality of the situation was grim. Most of the beds, vacated to accommodate injured passengers and crew, would not be needed.

The dedication shown by medical staff was not forgotten by the Manx people. Two young nurses received the exciting news that they had been chosen to go on a trip to the Isle of Man as a reward. It was a wonderful surprise! During their week on the Island, transport was provided by a taxi firm who may have lost one of their relatives in the tragedy. They attended a show at the Villa Marina and visited the town hall, where they were received by the mayor. A warm welcome greeted them everywhere they went.

Having required a blood transfusion, while in intensive care, Mr Kennish felt that he was "part" of the town of Bolton. I can understand that. Although I've joked that my love for the Isle of Man

stems from the "Manx" blood I received after the fire, I really do feel
a deep connection with the Island and Douglas in particular. When
I arrive in the capital, it's like coming home. I've never felt that way
before. I've lost so many years because I feared the past. Too late, I
discovered that the only way to overcome fear is to confront it; but
I'm thankful for all the wonderful trips I had before fate waded in
again.

I've learnt from Winter Hill, Summerland and other tragedies,
that people grieve in different ways. There is no set time to *get over*
a traumatic event. I used to be very upset when people said it was
time to put the fire behind me. It isn't a case of getting over it or
reaching a stage when it can be forgotten. It's about finding a way to
live with what has happened; a way to live in peace. It's finding the
courage to do what it takes to get to that point.

My dad was beside himself with excitement when his dream of
taking us to the Isle of Man came true. Arthur Tonkin, managing
director of Ramsey Motors, had planned a lovely day out for loyal
customers. The good intentions of both men ended in disaster.
Arthur's daughter, Elizabeth, felt the need to visit the place where
the plane went down; but four decades passed before she had the
strength to do so. She hadn't realised that in Bolton and Horwich,
the Manxmen have never been forgotten, and that meant so much
to her. On the fortieth anniversary, Elizabeth laid a wreath on Winter
Hill in tribute to her dear father, who was lost to her on that far off
February day.

Memorials aren't always erected immediately after a tragic event,
nor are they always placed at the site. Some people like to attend a
public ceremony on the anniversary, while others prefer to reflect
in private. A lady, who narrowly escaped the fire in Summerland,
told me that she travels to the coast and walks for miles each second
day of August. Another Summerland survivor buys fresh flowers for
her home. Both feel unfounded guilt because they survived. They
aren't the only ones who feel this way; and all of us are vulnerable.

It is important not to judge. Each person must do what is right for them.

Jennifer Fleet was asked to unveil a memorial plaque at Ronaldsway Airport, an event attended by the families and friends of the men who died.

The original intention had been to place the memorial in the Boardroom at Ronaldsway, but Fred Kennish stepped in to ensure that it was displayed outside. I've only seen it in a photograph, but the plaque, set into a stone, seems similar in size to the first Summerland memorial, erected in 1998.

There was no memorial on the Isle of Man for those who perished in the Winter Hill air disaster, until the plaque was installed at Ronaldsway. This also occurred in 1998, forty years after the devastating event. One of the bereaved reckoned that something should have been done much sooner, as quite a number of those widowed by the crash had passed away. Survivor Fred Kennish believed that he should have been consulted about the memorial. He felt helpless when approached by relatives of the victims because he had no information to give them. Mention was also made of the difficulty there may have been for the person tasked with organising the ceremony, as he was only a child when the tragedy occurred.

Fred, who was given the honour of Freeman of the Borough of Douglas in 2005, summed up his feelings about the tribute to the men who lost their lives, "…all I wanted was a plaque in a public garden to the memory of the people who left that morning."

When I look at our beautiful Summerland memorial in the Kaye Garden, I remember the words of the brave Manxman who suffered so much but was determined to ensure that his comrades are never forgotten.

There was no counselling for those affected by the Winter Hill tragedy, just as there wouldn't be after the Summerland fire, fifteen years later. Fortunate were the survivors and bereaved with loving families and supportive friends to help them through the tough times; and to put a comforting arm around their shoulders when jagged memories threatened to cut them to the bone.

Some people can speak of their traumatic experiences immediately, but for others it is much more difficult, and their pain is often bottled up for a very long time.

While the scars of the Summerland fire were still raw, a Horwich policeman, who assisted at the temporary morgue, after the plane crash, was settling into his new position on the Isle of Man. When he retired in 1988, Don Hulme had risen to the rank of Detective Chief Inspector. Over the years, he had become acquainted with quite a few relatives of those who perished in the air disaster; he even worked with some of them. Yet, in all that time, he never mentioned the part he played; he couldn't. It wasn't until the fortieth anniversary that Don finally broke his silence.

Something the late Mayor of Douglas, Fred Kennish, said about the tragedy at Winter Hill burrowed its way into my heart, as my dad used the same expression. I heard him say it about Summerland, when pressed for information. It stuck in my mind because the fire was so rarely spoken of. He said that Summerland was just "one of those things."[41]

***

[This chapter is dedicated to the victims and survivors of the Winter Hill air disaster and to everyone who loved them.][42]

Chapter 6: Sunshine and Shadows
Part 1 – Hopes and Fears

We didn't have a large garden, when we were children; but in our minds it was vast – full of all kinds of creatures; the setting of many adventures. Mum and Dad loved it too, and my sister and I were careful not to spoil the tidy lawn and colourful beds while we played. The swing was used for competitions. (The winner being the person who jumped from the greatest height when it was in motion.) In fine weather, we'd drape the frame with sheets and have tea in our tent. It gave up the ghost eventually, too unsafe for its true purpose. I was a teenager then, and I'd sometimes sit on the warped seat thinking. The rusty chain made me feel sad. The frame had been painted several colours over the years, but the rust had eaten through that too. Above my head, yellow and blue had merged into green, red over blue looked purple in places. There was even a spot of orange. It was a ruined rainbow, and soon it would be gone.

***

Since I was a little girl, I've thought of March 1st as the "crow's wedding day." My dad took great delight in announcing the date when I arrived downstairs for breakfast! I'd rush into the garden to search for the "bride" and "groom," but apart from a faithful robin, perched on the fence, there was nothing. The robin had its head tilted, watching for worms; not in the least bit alarmed by my presence or inclined to move. I was full of excitement because it meant that my birthday was only a week away. March was my special month. It was also a special month for my father and younger sister. Dad would celebrate his birthday a few days after mine, but Lynda had to wait for more than a fortnight. He said we were all "mad March hares," and told us about real hares having boxing matches in the spring. I had a secret hope of seeing them engaged in this sport, during which I fully believed they would be wearing proper boxing gloves. I also yearned to see the crows in their wedding finery. The fact that I saw neither didn't spoil the magic in the slightest.

I had a party at home on my fifth birthday. The swing was my special present. I soared higher and higher, enjoying the exhilaration. I felt smart in my white blouse and yellow tank top, waiting for my friends to arrive. Party food was laid out on the dining room table. There was a space for the cake, which would appear when our ice cream and jelly were finished. We played indoor games after we had eaten. It was dark outside by then. I knew what was in "pass the parcel," but ripped off the paper enthusiastically, then feigned surprise when the contents were revealed!

Like all good things, my party was over too soon. When I think of it now, I remember an abundance of yellow: my tank top, the swing and yellow icing on my cake, although Easter was late that year. Yellow flowers made the front window cheerful and welcomed visitors to our home. We went to the Isle of Man five months later. For a long time, every day was grey after that.

In 2018, on the day before my fiftieth birthday, I glanced out of the bedroom window when making the bed. Something caught my eye, and I stopped what I was doing to have a better look. To my surprise, there was a large hare sitting at the bottom of the orchard. It was the first time I had spotted one in our area.

We are paid regular visits by a fox and a family of squirrels, and an old badger lumbered to and from his sett until he was killed on the road. He followed the same path for a long time before his luck ran out. I was out for a walk one evening, when dusk was rapidly turning to darkness. I heard his nails skittering on the tarmac, in panic, as he frantically tried to escape. He wouldn't have known that I meant him no harm. I saw the low outline of his shape, when he brushed against my foot, and drew in my breath. It was more than I could have hoped for. A few months later, we were passing the same spot in the car, and there he was, on the verge; magnificent as ever, even in death. Grass grew over the front of his home, and I tried not to look – it was upsetting to see it that way. I'd stood there often, before his demise, and pictured him snug in his earthy burrow, hidden from sight. Men used to come with their dogs; just to get the scent they said. I was able to save him then, but in the end, old age got the better of him.

I thought of Dad, when I saw the hare. I hadn't been looking forward to my "big" birthday. Both Dad and Gran were gone. My family waited for a few weeks before surprising me with a party, when I least expected it. I wish now that I'd celebrated with less restraint. My toddler grandson's little cheeks were puffed up to help Nannie blow out her candles! I should have carried out the task with gusto, but something didn't feel right. As soon as those candles were extinguished, the countdown had begun. The minutes were ticking away. The hands of the clock were moving towards a time later that year, and when they reached it, normal life, for me, would end. All the terrible dreams I'd had would become reality. Every twinge that was dismissed and all the feelings of panic – they were there to warn. I would have to claw my way to my next birthday. The hare had come to give me strength. I was going to need it.

***

As March 2017 ended, the days began to lengthen. Jaunty daffodils bobbed their heads at dainty primroses along the lane that leads to our home. Snowy lambs frisked energetically in nearby fields, but I felt very weary. All my days were taken up with Summerland and a good portion of each night too. It was 3:00 am or after, when exhaustion won, and I had to stop typing. After a few hours, I'd reach for my laptop again. That was the pattern of my life until June, when the finishing line was in sight.

I didn't go to bed at all during the last forty-eight hours of work on my manuscript. I was close to the end, despite many hurdles and my fear that something bad would happen before I finished. I couldn't stop! Finally, it was done.

The television, which was usually on all day and part of the night, for company, was silent. It had powered off the previous evening, when I'd been so engrossed in my task that I hadn't noticed. Although, I generally work better with a bit of noise in the background.

When I was studying for exams in my teenage years, Mum would tell me to turn off my music. She didn't understand that it was too quiet without it. Like many of my friends, I did my O level revision to the memorable hits of 1984, which always sounded best turned up full blast. Two years later, with A levels looming, the music was even louder! Then the worry was over, very suddenly it seemed. The exams were finished and so was school. We were light-hearted when we set off for home, some girls in their own cars. "I'll ring you soon," had to be yelled in order to be heard above the beeping horns. I travelled by bus, and as we passed sights that had become so familiar, reality dawned: it was the last time I would make the journey on a daily basis. Life was changing. Lots of my friends had holidays booked. They were looking forward to a few months of freedom, before the serious business of employment or further education began. I hadn't made any plans.

I thought back to the excitement of the sixth form formal, the talk of dresses, make-up and hair appointments. The venue was the Europa Hotel, in Belfast – then called the Forum, after a change of ownership. It became the Europa once more, in the autumn of 1986, a few months after I left school.

Like Summerland, the hotel opened in 1971. It was not without its sorrows either. A base for journalists through Northern Ireland's "Troubles," the landmark building, on Great Victoria Street, became known as the "most bombed hotel in Europe." However, despite this, the Europa is still standing and has welcomed many famous people, including an American president and his wife. In fact, a suite is named in their honour.[43]

My anxiety prevented me from participating in a very special event. If I hadn't been aware that the hotel was a casualty of Ulster's unrest, I would probably have attended my Formal and had a good time with friends. I felt left out – as if I was being punished. It was a feeling that I would experience often.

Relief that my task had ended was tinged with sadness. *Made in Summerland* had been my constant companion for several years. No matter where I was, or what I was doing, since I began to write, I was always somewhat distracted by thoughts of the chapter I was working on.

Beyond the kitchen window, on that June morning, magpies were squabbling over the scraps that I'd thrown out when dawn was trailing lazy fingers across the sky. Apart from my black and white friends, who persisted with their irate clacking, nothing stirred at Tullycarn. The big house, fifty yards away, childhood home of my husband and his siblings, would once have been full of activity as the busy farming day commenced. Early to bed and early to rise was the motto of that generation.

I stood a little while, gazing out. One of the cats was making her way up the lane, head down, embarrassed and dejected by her lack of a gift for me. On a summer evening, the previous year, I heard her crying at the door. I was reading at the time and got up absentmindedly to let her in. Suddenly, Cushla had my full attention as did the tiny mouse she dropped at my feet. I hadn't realised that something so small could move so quickly. Despite my lack of enthusiasm, and the fact that her trophy was restored to its natural habitat, she persisted in her quest for a suitable token of appreciation. I greeted her warmly and provided compensation for her fruitless endeavours. Afterwards, she flopped into bed to sleep the day away and dream of things that might have been. There would be no sleep for me.

As my husband and I hadn't been away together for several years, I'd booked a short break to coincide with the completion of *Made in Summerland*. Of course, when I made the reservation in the spring, I hadn't known that I'd be working on it until the last minute! Beside the packed cases sat a bulky brown envelope, ready to be posted at the beginning of our journey.

The lady in the post office asked what my package contained. I considered the answer I might have given her – more than four decades of pain, of sorrow, guilt and shame; friendships forged through tragedy, kindness, compassion and hope. In the end I said only two words: a manuscript. She asked no further questions, and I watched as she fixed a large stamp to the top right-hand corner; then it was gone.

The relief was immense. I could really breathe again and finally look forward to a few days of relaxation. I was mercifully oblivious to the fact that something had already occurred; something that would rock my world for a second time.

Chapter 6: Sunshine and Shadows
Part 2 – Popcorn and Fairy Floss

Not long into our journey on 14th June 2017, I felt very sleepy and struggled to stay awake. That changed when we reached Portstewart, one of our favourite places in Northern Ireland. I was fully alert as we parked near the harbour and more than ready for a walk in the fresh air. I could feel the strain of the past months easing with every step I took.

We went into Morelli's for coffee on our way back, and the tempting aromas persuaded us to have an early lunch.

Waiting in the queue to be served, I thought of all the times Dad had taken my children to Morelli's for one of their famous ice creams. He loved being a grandfather.

My aunt had a caravan in the Skerries Holiday Park, on the outskirts of Portrush (an eight-minute drive from Portstewart), and she was keen for other family members to avail of it. Mum and Dad often took the children to stay for a few days, when it was free. They would do the same things my sister and I enjoyed during trips to the North Coast long ago. We didn't venture any further than that familiar and much-loved location in the first few years after the fire.

My children have such happy memories. They'd wake up to the delicious smell of their granddad cooking breakfast. He had already been for a long walk by then. The newness of the day, and the solitude that accompanies it, greatly appealed to him. An early morning walk was one of his holiday rituals. Even though Dad was a sociable person, those few hours alone with nature were precious. He was in awe of our beautiful world and said there would be plenty of time to sleep later…

As Dad was serving the food, he'd outline exciting plans for the hours ahead. During those halcyon days, they went fishing in rock pools with nets newly bought from a little shop in Portballintrae. Refreshments were purchased then too. Dad was infinitely patient. Arguments over lemonade for the ice cream floats were solved by buying small bottles of each flavour, which pleased everybody, though one big bottle would have been more economical. Mum picked a comfortable spot to read her book. Then the serious business of fishing got underway!

The catch was always meagre and on no occasion resembled a fish. Generally, long strands of seaweed and shells, and sometimes a tiny crab were brought to Nanny Moo to be admired! They were much exclaimed over and thought of. Lips dropped when requests to bring the treasures home were denied. Their grandad always had an explanation ready: a mummy crab searching for her baby or a sea creature that was depending on the kelp for its dinner!

A trip to the *Giant's Causeway* was always a firm favourite. Their enjoyment of the spectacular hexagonal-shaped basalt columns was enhanced by their grandfather's tales of warring giants. I yearn for the days of my childhood, when I delighted in those stories too. I longed for the giant to make an appearance, to reclaim his missing boot or to sit at his organ and play a tune. I wasn't overawed by the size of his chair. I knew I was safe because Daddy was holding my hand.

On the drive back to the Skerries, after an ice cream supper, all was quiet in the back seat. Tired eyes watched the sun drop slowly into the sea. Sleep was close at hand.

I remember the last time we were all in Morelli's together. It was before Dad became ill. Lynda was a mum then too, and her little boy was with us. Dad was in his element! He smiled at the children indulgently as orders were placed for a variety of sundaes, instead of the usual "kids" ice creams, and when they said that they would *definitely* be able to eat them! He only ordered a cup of tea for himself and responded reassuringly when asked, "Are you not having one Granda?" He knew there would be a surfeit of ice-cream later, in the guise of "We left you share!"

Knickerbocker Glory was on the menu too. The elaborate dessert reminds me of a special moment when I was about eight years old. The memory still brings a tear to my eye.

In the *Arcadia*, situated on the East Strand in Portrush, tall glasses, full of ice cream, fruit and syrup were being placed on the table next to ours. I longed for one. The beach café was one of my favourite places in the seaside town. A ballroom was added to the building in the 1950s, and I remember looking at old photographs, which show mum and her friends standing close to it. I always meant to ask her if she'd gone to a dance there. Though, I am almost certain she did, as she told us she went to all the dances!

Lynda and I climbed the steps from the small beach beneath where the *Arcadia* stood, hungry and thirsty after the hard work of building sandcastles. Once seated in the café, with Mum and Dad, we let our imaginations wander. It was easy to pretend that we were on a boat because of the panoramic view. On such a day, we were waiting patiently for our child-sized desserts to arrive, when to my amazement a waitress stopped at our table with one of those wonderful concoctions, that I'd envied so much! I thought she had made a mistake, but then I saw the smile on Dad's face! I could barely believe it was for me. I stared at it, mesmerised. There was even a cherry perched on the whipped cream topping. I wasn't fond of cherries, but it was essential to complete the effect. Strawberry sauce, between each layer, made little pathways as it trickled down the inside of the glass. I felt like crying: warm tears of happiness because I had the best daddy in the whole world! I didn't eat all the Knickerbocker Glory or even come close to finishing it. Lynda shook her head, when I looked to her for salvation. Dad laughed. He had known I wouldn't be able to manage it, but he'd ordered it anyway, to please me, for that is the kind of person he was.

There have been many changes in our lives, since that family outing to Morelli's. Dad lived long enough to welcome his eighth grandchild; and, even though he was very ill, we managed a brief visit to Portrush four months after her birth.

A highlight of that trip was a visit to *Barry's* amusements. My children and eldest nephew were braver than I was as a child and attempted most of the rides. I've never forgotten the fear I felt on a miniature version of the fun park's famous rollercoaster. I had to endure the whole experience, and I was considerably green about the gills by the end. I knew for certain as I staggered towards my waiting parents, with a beaming Lynda by my side, that I'd never join a queue of youngsters waiting to check their height on a board in front of the *Big Dipper*. Many of them stood on tiptoe to appear taller. I wouldn't suffer the disappointment of being turned away. Just looking up at the cars, full of screaming people, made my stomach lurch.

I had no reservations about climbing aboard the *Ghost Train*, however, and barely noticed the spectres that sprang up, unexpectedly, or the macabre shrieks and puffs of chill air. I was fascinated by the track's twists and turns and wished I could see the layout with the lights on.

I thoroughly enjoyed the "Bumper Cars" too. That name seemed so much more appropriate than *Dodgems*, as many of their young drivers seemed to want to collide with, rather than steer away from the other cars. I was in the minority, preferring to avoid a collision and the accompanying jolt. It was the same with the *Ghost Train*! When the carriage burst through the swing doors at the end of the ride, I sprang out before the next one through had a chance to bang into us!

The mechanical arms of the *Cyclone* flung its chairs towards big windows that overlooked the Atlantic. It seemed for a moment that one of them would break away and end up among the crashing waves! When the action was repeated, close to where I was standing, causing the seat's white-knuckled occupants to slide to one end, I jumped back a little. Although I told myself there was no danger, it wasn't enough to convince me to participate, and my feet remained firmly planted on the ground!

I didn't have a chance to ride the hobbyhorses in Summerland, but they were a firm favourite at *Barry's*. The colourful steeds, much loved, bobbed up and down with smiling children on their backs. Mummies and daddies stood next to toddlers, in case they slipped from the glossy saddle when the carousel picked up speed.

I recently asked my youngest daughter what she remembers most about the popular venue. "The smell," she replied, before concluding, "It just smelt like *Barry's*; nowhere else ever smelt like that!"

The *Dodgems* are silent now, the smell of popcorn is gone, but I can still hear the music of the carousel in my mind and picture the bobbing horses, teeth bared benignly. I see my children, too, small hands waving in excitement. Their grandad is with them, a protective arm around each little figure, keeping them safe. He did the same with my sister and me, when we were young. Fate stepped in, most cruelly, and made him feel he'd failed us. Dad, you didn't fail! You've always been our hero![44]

During our last trip to the north coast with Dad, he promised his grandchildren all the treats they could manage. He would be going into hospital soon after. It was almost the end of the season and the final visit for many families, before the days grew shorter and the classroom beckoned. The sun was still high in the sky when we walked back to the cars, but for Dad the shadows were already lengthening.

Despite my good intentions, I yielded to temptation on the day I celebrated the book being finished. It wasn't difficult to persuade Robert to join me. On my way to the counter to place our dessert order, I'd spotted some framed prints; and when the last of my ice cream and chocolate sauce were scraped from the bottom of the dish, I walked over to have a look.

There, on a back wall, in the bright sea-front restaurant, was the history of the Morelli family business. Fascinated, I started to read.

An elderly man came to stand by my side and began to chat. Normally, I would have enjoyed the conversation, but I was engrossed in the story before me. Robert joined us, and the man happily transferred his attention. Names were mentioned and places familiar to both, even though our homes are far apart!

Suddenly, three words sprang out, and I no longer heard what my husband and his new friend were saying…

At the Manx Museum in Douglas, a man studied the roll of those who had been internees on the Island during the Second World War. It was an emotional moment, evoking, as it did, many memories of a sad and worrying time in his life; but it was also a time of comradeship, of pulling together and making the best of things. That man was Angelo Morelli. He was on the Isle of Man to be filmed for a documentary, which would tell the story of his long and interesting life. His story is one of determination, of hard work and ambition, of triumph over adversity. It is a story of love and hope. Most of all, it is a story of success.

When Angelo arrived in Ireland with his father, in 1916, it was a baptism of fire for them both. Though, if the situation had been otherwise, he may have stayed in Dublin city, and his story could have been very different.

Barbato Morelli, one of nine brothers, had watched some of his siblings depart from the little hamlet of San Andrea in beautiful Casalattico, to search for employment. The bit of land owned by the family wasn't sufficient to give them all a living. Bidding farewell to their loved ones, they left the shelter of the mountains for an uncertain future. Barbato, who lost a leg to infection, married a local girl, and the couple became parents to a little boy, Angelo.

Angelo's mother was eager to provide for her husband and child, and in 1915 she had the chance to do so. Maria-Celeste, aided by her brother, opened her own shop in Dublin. After a year, she had earned enough to send for Barbato and nine-year-old Angelo. Unfortunately, their arrival coincided with a period of turbulence in the city. Just a short time later, parents and son retreated to the basement of the shop in terror, while the Easter Rising raged around them. Emerging a week later, much distressed by their ordeal, it was decided that young Angelo would leave Dublin for Northern Ireland, where he would stay with his uncle and aunt. The move would eventually prove fortuitous for him.

Peter (Pietro) Morelli had started his own business after gaining experience working in his brother, *Joe's* (Giuseppe) café in Ballymena. From his premises on Stone Row, Coleraine, Peter provided the people of the town with tasty fish and chips. Ice cream was on the menu too. Love followed. Peter married a local girl, Annie, and they worked hard and companionably together. Then, in 1914, Peter's ambition was realised when he purchased the *Ice Palace* on Portstewart promenade. It was a huge success.

At the end of three years of education, Barbato took his son home to Italy. When Angelo finished his studies, it was clear that he, too, must leave Casalattico. Soon, he was back in Coleraine. Peter had a job for Angelo. His new place of employment was the *Ice Palace*. The young man toiled tirelessly towards his goal, wanting to make his parents proud, and at last he was in the position to buy the business, now re-christened the *Lido*. However, Angelo's life was one ingredient short of perfection!

In the church of San Barbato, a commanding presence in the "piazza" of Casalattico, with its unusual tower, Angelo Morelli married his childhood sweetheart. He brought his beautiful bride Anastasia back to Portstewart, where they took up residence over the shop. Their lives would not be without twists and turns, but their devotion to each other would carry them through.

Anastasia quickly became acquainted with her new environment. Her warm personality endeared her to everyone she met. The shop was always busy. When Guido, the couple's youngest child, was born in 1935, Barbato and Maria-Celeste, travelled from Italy to see the latest arrival. Their presence eased the pressure for their son and daughter-in-law in the hectic summer season. Sadly, it was during this visit that tragedy struck. Barbato died unexpectedly. He was just sixty-one.

In 1939, Angelo, Anastasia and little Guido travelled to Casalattico to visit Maria-Celeste and their two older boys, who had returned with their grandmother following her husband's death. Although Italy was still at peace at that stage, it was clear that trouble was brewing elsewhere. Their journey back to Portstewart was fraught. It was an omen of imminent change and frightening times to come.

The internees of the Palace camp, on Douglas seafront, had a picturesque view. It was particularly enjoyable in summer, when sunshine increased activity along the promenade, providing entertainment for the men detained behind barbed wire.

Fate had tried to place Angelo Morelli in a position of peril, but fortune intervened.

After being removed from his home as an *enemy alien*, he was taken to Crumlin Road Gaol and from there to a camp in Lancashire, where there were thousands of other men of several nationalities. Poor Angelo endured deplorable conditions, far from his beloved family; anxiety and uncertainty were ever present. Then, finally, there was action. Names were read out, and when Angelo heard his name, he joined the group he was directed to. However, there had been a mix up. His name was called a second time, and he was sent back to where he had started. Angelo's group would be travelling to the Isle of Man, and the group he belonged to, briefly, due to a clerical error, was destined for Canada, on board the SS *Arandora Star*.

On 2nd July 1940, the liner, not long into her journey to Newfoundland, was struck by a torpedo. More than eight hundred people died, including the ship's master, Captain E.W. Moulton, a number of his officers and other members of the crew.

Once settled on the Island, the men heard from home at last.

Food parcels began to arrive, which were very welcome. Although they had enough to eat, the men missed the variety and flavour of their Italian food. Generally, they kept the much-anticipated treats for themselves. Angelo, however, a generous and considerate person, shared the contents of a large parcel from his dear wife. It arrived just before his birthday. As well as containing food that he loved, there was also some Italian wine. It called for a party! Among the men in Angelo's camp were Italian chefs, who had previously been employed in a London restaurant. They conjured up a feast. A humorous menu, made by the other men and signed by each of them, was presented as a birthday card. It remains a treasured possession within the Morelli family.

Angelo found Douglas much changed, when he returned in 2002. Pit marks in the road were the only reminder of the barbed wire enclosure, though the Grasmere Boarding House, his home for several years, was still there. Furniture from the Grasmere and other boarding houses along the sea front, had been placed in storage for the duration of the war. At the end of the promenade, the ballroom of Derby Castle was temporary home to much of that furniture. In 1940, it would have been impossible to believe that the venue, once so popular with Victorian holidaymakers, would be replaced, three decades later, with an acrylic clad entertainment centre; "the first of its kind in the world."

The new Summerland building was leased by *Trust Houses Forte* (THF), which eventually became the Forte *Group*. One of the names on the menu gifted to Angelo was that of an acquaintance from Casalattico. His name was Charles Forte, founder of the group, and Chief Executive Officer of THF when the Douglas complex opened to the public in 1971.

Baron Forte was ninety-eight when he died at the end of February 2007, less than two weeks after Angelo Morelli, who passed away in the town of his birth, eight months short of his one hundredth birthday. At the end of the same year, Summerland architect, James

Philipps Lomas, died at the age of ninety-three. When just a few hours of 2007 remained, the bottom fell out of our world. Dad was seventy when we lost him, and he had so much more living to do. All four men have had an effect on me, each in a different way.

When I visit Morelli's now, I think of the moment Angelo was reunited with his beloved wife. The family were all together again in 1945, when the older boys returned home. The business, which Anastasia kept going through the war years, thrived.

Gone are the days when blocks of ice travelled by train from Belfast, before making their way to the shop on a tram, but the Morelli family work as hard as ever. Eleven decades of tradition are behind each delicious creamy treat. That thought fills me with emotion, and I know that if my dear dad were still here, he would feel exactly as I do.[45]

***

There's a little shop in Portstewart that reminds me of childhood trips to the shore. Novelties hang in the doorway along with buckets and spades and beach balls – a colourful display! Rainbow windmills spin furiously, catching the eye of tiny passers-by. Plump baby fingers point in vain. Their infant carriages trundle on, leaving the moment behind.

Sticks of peppermint and fruit-flavoured rock are run through with the name of the town. As youngsters, we could make a bar last for ages, licking it into a point until the lettering was exposed. Hot hands made the labels hard to peel off and little bits stuck to our tongues. We always bought fudge for Gran and some Dulse for an elderly aunt. A sign on the souvenir shop proclaims that both are for sale inside.

The seaweed snack reminds me of Ballycastle and stalls at the *Ould Lammas Fair*. Dad would have turn after turn throwing hoops to win prizes for us, but a doll I had my eye on evaded him. He spent more than the cost of the doll before I begged him to stop! A bag of *Yellowman* compensated the loss. Chewy honeycomb clung to my teeth. Candy Floss did that too, but I didn't mind. It was my favourite seaside treat; and if I had known its other name, I would have loved it even more! They spun it in front of you, then, a magical process without doubt. It comes in bags and tubs too, nowadays, though that isn't the same at all!

When we passed the little shop on the prom, after our visit to Morelli's in 2017, I decided we would return with our grandchildren. I knew it was somewhere they'd love. Time slipped by, then fate intervened, frustrating all of my plans.

***

It was late afternoon, when Robert and I pulled up outside our hotel in the Roe Valley Country Park, Limavady. The setting was described as tranquil, which we both enjoy, and I certainly needed after the pressure of completing the book. Robert had passed the entrance to the resort several times, when working in the area, and mentioned how nice it would be to stay there. We had both been looking forward to our minibreak. Yet, neither of us felt excited when we arrived, despite the beautiful scenery. I hoped it wasn't an omen.

I usually unpack straight away, but lack of sleep in those final days of editing the manuscript had tired me out. When staying in a hotel alone, the television is rarely on, but I wanted to see the evening news, to catch up with what was happening in the world. Robert switched it on. I gazed through the window, while waiting for images to appear on the screen. Two men were enjoying a leisurely game of golf beneath a mellow sun. The room filled with the newsreader's voice, tearing my attention away from the restful sight.

How can I explain my feelings about what I saw? I was transfixed by the image of a blazing building! *Cladding* – the word snapped me out of my trance-like state. It was Summerland again. I felt physically sick. Although I vowed, before I left home, that I would leave Summerland behind for a few days, I reached for my bag. In the bottom lay the *Report of the Summerland Fire Commission*, next to my notebook. I told my husband that I'd forgotten to take it out. The truth was, I brought it to read the recommendations, to reassure myself that a fire like the one at Summerland could never happen again…

Grenfell is a name I was unfamiliar with, until I read the poem, *If I Should Die*, and discovered that it was written by a lady called Joyce Grenfell. It was one of the secular readings at the service to mark the demolition of the Summerland building. I could never have imagined, when I decided to include a verse in *Made in Summerland*, that the name *Grenfell* would shortly evoke horror every time it was mentioned.

I did my best to be positive after finding out about the terrible event in London. When I tried to sleep, I saw figures at the windows of the burning tower block, waiting in desperation to be saved. For some, there was no hope. I had an episode of sleep walking, which I thought was something I had overcome. I knew that the blaze would bring back dreadful memories for those affected by other fire disasters. I realised that some who had survived Summerland or who had been bereaved by it, would be distraught, and I began to fret.

The fire alarm going off, unexpectedly, was the death knell of any chance there might have been to salvage some enjoyment from the remainder of our stay.

Chapter 7: Haunted by the Past

On 16th June, Robert and I checked out of the Roe Park hotel. It hadn't been the relaxing break we had hoped for. We stopped for a while at Benone Strand, where we'd spent many enjoyable days when our children were young. Back then, the car was full of the paraphernalia required for a successful trip to the beach. On the homeward journey, wet hair, damp towels and sopping swimsuits steamed up the windows; whereupon little fingers got busy writing names and drawing pictures. The years flew by, and all too soon those happy times were over. We felt bereft.

When our grandchildren started to arrive, we had a purpose once more. The adventure was beginning again.

It was on Benone strand, that we had introduced our first granddaughter to the highs and lows of building sandcastles. We shared her delight when the *castle* came out of its mould without mishap and in her dismay when the sea water, she had carried so carefully, disappeared when tipped into the moat. We remembered how upset we felt when we were children, and the same thing happened to us. It was even more distressing to watch someone jump on your masterpiece, while you watched helplessly as the car moved slowly away.

On that Friday afternoon, in 2017, I needed a walk in the bracing sea air to ease my mind. In the past, the beach, with its incredible background of mountain and cliffs, never failed to lift my spirits, even in winter. However, on that bright summer day my heart was heavy. When we turned to retrace our steps, leaving a breath-taking view of the Donegal coastline behind us, Mussenden Temple, on its distant, lofty perch, captured our attention.

The unusual stone building, with its domed roof, had fascinated the children. They beseeched us to take them to have a look inside, and we always said that we would go next time. But the promised visit didn't take place until our youngest child was a teenager, and the others had flown the nest. It was very busy that day. We didn't see all the attractions and vowed to go again. Mum was with us too, and she thoroughly enjoyed the outing. As with most things related to Ireland's history, she already knew the story of Downhill Demesne and the cliff-top rotunda – inspired by the Temple of Vesta – and was able to tell us about it. We didn't make it back together. Something always got in the way; and that haunts me.

Frederick Augustus Hervey, born in Suffolk in 1730, was unusual in that he had inherited his title as a third son. Both of his older brothers were Earl of Bristol before him. George, the elder of the two, in his capacity as Lord Lieutenant of Ireland, bestowed the title Bishop of Derry on Frederick: it was a position that paid well. When George died, Augustus John was next in line. Following his untimely death, Frederick, still in his thirties, became a very wealthy man – having inherited his brothers' estates as well as the title. The new 4th Earl of Bristol, referred to as the Earl Bishop, was known for his great benevolence. Frederick Hervey really embraced his role and took the people of Ireland to his heart.

Having a keen interest in the subject, he was immediately entranced by the volcanic landscape of the area we know as the Giant's Causeway. Frederick Hervey received recognition for his great contribution to the causeway, both for his work and for drawing attention to it. People come from all over the world to enjoy the phenomenal sight.

It wasn't easy for the Earl Bishop to make frequent trips to the north coast to indulge his passion because of the distance from his diocese. This prompted him to look for land where he could have a summer house built. Downhill was perfect. The bishop's "holiday home" gradually expanded until it became a magnificent manor house (sadly now a ruin) of sufficient size to accommodate Hervey's treasured works of art.

In the mid-1780s, the Earl Bishop commissioned a "temple," which would be used as an additional library to house some of his extensive collection of books. It would also be a retreat for his cherished cousin, when she came to visit. Perhaps, if the social whirl became too much for Frideswide Mussenden, she might slip away to enjoy the solitude and the soothing sound of the sea.

On the day of our visit to the National Trust Property, I wasn't brave enough to stand close to the windows and look down on the beach, more than one hundred feet below, as others were doing. I admired the scenery standing some way back, instead, and hoped that a train would pass through the tunnel in the cliff beneath us!

The great height, the expanse of sky and the movement of the water, brought Summerland, on the night of the fire, to mind. I recalled that brief time when all was well, and our little family were on the top terrace taking in the magnificent view of Douglas Bay; so much a part of the wondrous Summerland experience – just as the building's architects had intended.

In the late 1700s, Douglas was a village, and Castletown was the Island's capital. The Northern end of Douglas promenade was somewhat isolated, making it the perfect location for someone who liked to withdraw from the stresses and strains of life and perhaps do a spot of fishing! Around five years after the completion of the Earl Bishop's temple at Downhill, the Duke of Atholl's "retreat" was built. In the 1830s, he sold his land to a businessman from Lancashire. When Derby Castle (the Duke of Atholl also held the title, Earl of Derby) changed hands again, around forty years later, its new owner opened a hotel and leisure park.

Sadly, its popularity began to decline after the war. Tastes were changing. The package holiday meant foreign travel was now more affordable. Many, who would usually have been have setting off for locations around Great Britain, including the Isle of Man, were climbing the steps of a plane, sunshine bound. Something stupendous was needed to encourage people to spend their hard-earned pennies closer to home, where the weather can be unpredictable to say the least! Heads got together, and the Derby Castle Complex was demolished to make way for the future. The architects responsible for its replacement, visited Expo '67 in Montreal and were inspired by the American Pavilion. It wasn't quite in the same league as the temple in Tivoli but fascinating in its own way.

As we left the once elaborately decorated chamber, I imagined what it would be like to descend the stone steps in a long dress. There are handrails now, but they may have been a later addition like the classical style urn on the roof.

Two centuries of being battered by waves left the cliff needing urgent attention. The National Trust undertook work to ensure the building's safety in the last decade of the twentieth century. Its proximity to the edge makes it difficult to believe that a carriage could once be driven around it. On the day of our visit, quite a few people were standing close to the boundary wall. Mum joined them. She had no fear of heights. I watched as she looked towards Donegal, where she and Dad had enjoyed many holidays together, before fixing her gaze in the opposite direction. I knew she was thinking of the lovely family holiday in Castlerock, a long time ago: a time before the Summerland fire.

*＊＊

A little boy who grew up to be a famous author, also enjoyed holidays in Castlerock. I expect that he may have been just as enthralled by the coastal scenery as I was. The Giant's Causeway, Dunluce Castle and the ruins at Downhill could not fail to make a huge impression on a young lad from Belfast. C.S. Lewis greatly enriched my childhood through the mythical characters he created. I never gave up hope of finding snow-covered trees at the back of a wardrobe and the warm glow from a lamppost behind them, lighting the way to the enchanted land of Narnia.

I thoroughly enjoyed our annual Sunday school excursions to Portrush. My favourite part was the train journey, though as much as I enjoyed it, I would gladly have forfeited the pleasure for that tugging feeling experienced by the Pevensie children, before their return to Narnia – my dream destination. The years passed by, and my Narnia dream faded as the dreams of childhood do when we advance towards maturity. Soon, the gossamer strands that remained slipped through my fingers, despite my desperate attempts to cling on to them. I needed my dreams to cushion reality. It is only now that I realise that many of my dreams did come true, just not in the way I expected. On those long-ago Saturday mornings, when we clutched our buckets and spades, eagerly awaiting our first glimpse of the sea, Mum and Dad would point out places of interest. They flashed by in a blur of colour as the swift locomotive swallowed the miles. I had no idea then, that I *had* experienced Narnia. It was right there, all around me, in the wee country of my birth.

***

The rest of us admired the *temple's* exterior instead: the Corinthian columns, ornate carving, the frieze, with its Latin inscription, and the coat of arms above the door.

What excitement there would have been when the building began to take shape! (When the rotunda was not in use, the bishop had given local people permission to use the basement for religious ceremonies.) Frideswide, on her marriage to an older gentleman, changed her surname from Bruce to Mussenden. I'm sure that the Earl Bishop was counting the days until he could present his gift. Sadly, it wasn't to be.

Although the summer library housed his favourite tomes, it must have been a melancholy place for Frederick Hervey. I picture him, a subdued version of his former self, walking down the path from his beautiful home with the taste of sea salt on his lips; a breeze lifting strands of thinning hair. The keening gulls a reminder of his terrible loss. His visits to the library were few. A fire burnt constantly in the basement to keep the damp at bay, ensuring the books were perfectly preserved. But what use now? Their owner's heart had been torn in two. Frideswide would never sit in her beautiful retreat overlooking the wild Atlantic Ocean. She would never join her cousin in conversations about subjects of mutual interest. The young lady was not robust. She passed from this life just two years into her twenties, and the temple became her memorial.

As we walked away, replete with the past, I thought of the Latin inscription around the top of the building, just beneath the domed roof: "Suave mari magno turbantibus aequora ventis, e terra magnum alterius spectare laborem" – "'Tis pleasant, safely to behold from shore, the troubled sailor and hear the tempests roar." The quotation caused me to think of Summerland – of how the opposite was the case on the night of the fire. The inferno was spotted by a ship's captain, safe on his vessel in Douglas Bay, while those of us in the building were in terrible danger. The captain immediately contacted the coastguard, who alerted the emergency services. I don't agree with the words of Lucretius; but I believe they aren't intended literally and may have, in fact, a deeper meaning unconnected to the perils of the sea.[46]

***

Summerland is always with me; but these days we walk side by side. We understand each other now. However, on the beautiful beach at Benone, in mid-June 2017, it loomed above me, hand in hand with the new tragedy, at Grenfell.

I barely registered that we'd driven through Coleraine. Then my phone rang. It was Nicholas Tate from *Good Morning Ulster*. He asked if I would participate in an interview on Monday morning. I agreed. Difficult as it would be to talk about both Summerland

and Grenfell, I felt that it was something that I needed to do.

I was in turmoil. My hard-earned belief that lessons were learned from the tragic event that caused the greatest loss of life by fire, in peacetime Great Britain, until the Bradford football stadium disaster, was in tatters. Perhaps, I thought, things might have been different if Summerland had been more widely remembered and discussed. I mentioned the fun centre fire on a social media post about Grenfell, a few years ago. An architect responded. He hadn't heard of Summerland. In the dark days following the London blaze, I wondered what other people's thoughts were, particularly those who had been affected by the Isle of Man tragedy.

The dreadful fire at Grenfell Tower evoked painful memories for Joan Ford. She decided to record her thoughts because she considered the blaze at Summerland to be "similar." Mrs Ford's parents died when flames tore through the entertainment complex in Douglas.

"It hit me watching the coverage," Joan said. "How can it happen again?"

Robert and I met some other members of Joan's family in 2013. They, like us, had travelled to the Isle of Man to see the new memorial being unveiled on the fortieth anniversary. We chatted before the ceremony and introductions were made. When the names of those who lost their lives were read out, the anguish of the family was palpable. After the service, Joan's sister Jean and her brother-in-law Dennis Machen told us more about their own ordeal in Summerland. They also narrowly escaped death. Dennis dropped his two little girls from a balcony into the arms of a stranger. Jean, who knew some of the fire's other victims from Huddersfield, suffered burns and spent time in hospital.

Mrs Ford, from Newsome, a retired teacher, referred to the recommendations concerning cladding, which were reported after the Summerland fire, and questioned whether they had been adhered to. She felt that checks needed to be carried out on all buildings, particularly large ones, with regard to the materials used in their construction, escape routes and sprinkler systems.

Joan and Jean's parents, William and Phoebe Goldsmith, were sixty-two and sixty years old respectively at the time of their deaths.[47]

Memories came back to haunt Annette Swift too, when she watched the blazing tower on the news. She described how the fire in London "prompted" recollections of her terrifying experience in Summerland.

Annette contacted me the evening after Grenfell Tower was engulfed in flames, as she had come across my story when searching for information about the fun centre fire. She explained that she hadn't previously known how many people perished as a result of "that fateful day" in 1973. "We were so lucky," she said.

Realisation that something had gone badly wrong came when Annette, who had recently celebrated her twelfth birthday, and her cousin Kim were queuing for the Moonwalk – a type of bouncy castle – which was very popular with children who visited the entertainment complex. Perhaps they were keen to re-enact the unprecedented event that occurred a few years previously. Summerland's doors were opened exactly a decade after John Fitzgerald Kennedy spoke of his hope that man would land on the moon. Sadly, the American president didn't live to see his dream come to fruition.

When she noticed firemen, Annette knew they had to get out immediately. She grabbed hold of Kim and pulled her towards an exit. Their relief at having escaped, without injury, was short-lived. The girls' grandad had gone in to look for them. (Annette was on holiday with her grandparents, aunt, uncle and Kim). After a worrying wait, the family were reunited. In a nearby pub, blankets were wrapped around the shocked survivors, and they were given something to drink while the horror was ongoing a short distance away.

A fourteen-year-old girl, who attended the same school as Annette, perished in Summerland.

***

When we passed Juniper Hill Caravan Park, I recalled one particularly memorable Portrush holiday. It was August 1976. Dad took us to the grave of an unknown sailor nestled beneath the cliffs. I felt sad when I looked at the tiny posy of wildflowers that marked his final resting place. I thought of his mummy and daddy that day, and of how distressed they must have been when their son hadn't returned home. How awful that they had to live the rest of their lives without knowing what had happened to him. The most upsetting thing for me was the fact that he was nameless. There was no stone on his grave saying who he was. He had no identity.

As a child, I often looked at the graves in our churchyard when the Sunday service was over, and the adults were catching up on the week's news. Those belonging to children terrified me. I was fully aware that I had cheated death, just a few years before, and petrified by the thought that it might be waiting in the wings, ready to carry me off. That fear has never left me.

Dad used to say we should remember things so we could tell our own children about them. I vowed never to forget that lonely grave on the coastal path. Years later, it was the turn of my younger children to hear the story. They already knew about Dunluce Castle and the Spanish Armada. They also understood that although the Atlantic is mesmerizingly beautiful, it can be incredibly dangerous too. Another generation of our family is ready to pay homage to the unknown sailor, and it breaks my heart that someone else must take them there. Life, like the ocean, can be very cruel.

Our holiday, in 1976, began so promisingly. Lynda and I made friends with some other children. There are photos in which we have our arms around each other – flared trousers and striped socks were obviously the height of fashion! We are all smiling, not just for the camera but because we were genuinely happy. My scars often caused other children to shun me, and it was lovely to be accepted. Although the days were wonderful, I look back with the greatest feeling of nostalgia on those summer evenings.

When darkness fell, we were safe in our caravan. Dad lit the little gas globes on the walls, and the smell reminded me of the scullery in my great-granny's Belfast home. She died in early 1974; a few months after I got out of hospital. Her bedroom was on the top floor, and I couldn't climb all the stairs because of my grafts, which meant I didn't have a chance to say goodbye. Mum's heart was broken by her death. They were very close.

Mum was born in the three-storey house on Rathdrum Street, and spent most school holidays there. After securing a job in the city, she stayed during the week and many weekends as well. This was good company for Granny and helpful too, because she gave her a hand with the extra work caused by the lodgers (often young footballers). It was hard for Mum to lose the person who was like a second mother to her, so soon after our awful ordeal.

Annie Clements was a real character, and I wish she had lived longer. When she was a young girl, Annie wrote a poem in the back of her bible which was passed on to Mum. I read it many years ago and burst into tears. I'm crying now, thinking of it. She was afraid of being forgotten when she died!

Annie, one of a big family (her maiden name was Foote), often returned to her childhood home, Broughmore in Broomhedge, with her children: two sons and a daughter. There had been another little girl, Annie's firstborn, who sadly died in infancy. My mum was named in her honour. The older Clements boy loved those trips to the country. Nearly half a century later, the old farmhouse, where his mother was raised, became his home. It needed extensive modernisation, and although he was in his fifties by then, he carried out the strenuous work himself – keen to make it comfortable for his little family. That man was my grandfather, Ernie Clements. The move was to be a fresh start for him and Granny Jean after

Summerland, and the painful days of our convalescence at *Peartree Hill*, a few miles away.

I stayed with my grandparents as often as I could. My room was at the front of the house. The slightest movement made the big brass bed squeak. I loved to snuggle under the heavy woollen blankets and pretty bedspread; there were no bad dreams when I stayed at Broughmore. When I woke in the morning, I could see the little garden across the road, where, in the summer, Granny Annie's treasured roses bloomed without her.

***

As we drove along Portrush main street, in 2017, I thought about that childhood holiday again. Dad encouraged us to save our money for something special at the end of the week. It was a distraction from the sadness we felt because we would soon be homeward bound. He was a wise man. However, disaster struck on our way to Barry's one evening. I dropped the little round purse containing all my treasure into a grating. It could only happen to me! Dad tried in vain to fish it out with a stick. I cried as much for the purse, which had a picture of a fluffy cat on it – a gift from Gran – as for the loss of my holiday money, including a big shiny fifty pence piece. Dad promised to replace the lost funds, but I didn't need any money after all. The following day, we woke up to the news that a bomb had gone off in the town centre. My favourite shop had been destroyed. Mum called a lady who lived about half a mile from my grandparents, and she walked to their house to put their minds at rest. Grandad's reaction, when he heard about the bomb on the wireless, had been, "Oh no, not again." He hadn't known a moment's peace since we were caught up in the fire, and the latest catastrophe occurred on the heels of the third anniversary.

The following year was the Queen's Silver Jubilee. Security was tight as the royal yacht Britannia sailed along the coast. For my lovely grandad, there were no worries about us during that holiday. He had died on 16th August 1976, just thirteen days after the phone call which assured him that his precious family were safe. He was sixty years old. On the first anniversary of his death, I saw girls crying in school. When I asked them what was wrong, they told me it was because a famous singer they liked had died. That man was forty-two when he passed away – only a few years older than my daddy! My anxiety increased tenfold from that moment on.

**

Jacqueline Dimock lives in Australia, but at the time of the Summerland fire she was living in Douglas, Isle of Man, with her parents – the proprietors of the Seaforth Hotel – and her two younger sisters. The family had recently moved to the Island from Aberdeen.

Mr and Mrs Adams had an anguished wait to find out what had happened to Jacqueline, then aged twelve and Jill, nine, when the complex became an inferno.

The girls had gone to Summerland for the evening, and when the terrifying news reached their parents, Mr and Mrs Adams were frantic. During their short journey along the promenade, the fire had spread rapidly. Mrs Adams explained that "parts" of the building were "melting in flames." The scene of devastation made it impossible to believe that anyone could escape with their life. She and her husband feared the worst.

A gut-wrenching hour passed before the couple were reunited with their younger daughter. She was distraught. Separated from her older sister in the confusion, Jill had almost flung herself over a wall with a long drop on the other side. Tragedy was averted by the swift actions of a man who'd spotted the panicked youngster.

Jacqueline was discovered in a police car by her father. Thankfully, she too was unhurt, though badly shaken by her ordeal. The brave girl had smashed a window and aided the escape of other children. Information that she was able to give relating to when the fire began was passed on to the CID.

A few years ago, I chatted with Jacqueline about her traumatic experience, and I asked if moving away from the Isle of Man had helped in any way?

"You take your memories with you," she said. "Good and bad."[48]

Chapter 8: Lifebelt Twenty-Eight

The man with the camera gazes out to sea.
Who knows what thoughts are in his mind.
Perhaps there are no thoughts at all.
It's easier that way.

Teenagers laugh and jostle as they wait for spray
To drench them even more.
It's innocent fun – timeless.
Their voices carry along the promenade, full of life and hope.

A moonbeam makes a path across the rushing water of the bay.
The twinkling lights on the headland are like fallen stars.
I want to stay a while and drink it in, this bliss.
But he is waiting for me, where he always waits, at lifebelt twenty-
eight.

His hand on my shoulder is cold,
But his breath is hot as hell against my neck.
I do not look, I never have; yet, beneath the dark hood of his coat,
I know his eyes are blazing.

He guides me to the railings as he must.
The sea is angry now, lashing out at fate.
Beyond my line of sight, Manannan stands; Fragarach in his hand.
Enbarr rears impatiently, ready to cross the waves to carry me home.

I linger for a moment between worlds, eternity within my grasp.
A fragile hold on life is all I have. Life wins.
Alone again, I did not see him go.
But that's the way it is.

He leaves as silently as he comes.
The world is still the same:
A man with a camera gazing out to sea
And young folk laughing.

My husband drove me to Belfast, complaining mildly that we'd left home much too soon. It was Sunday, he pointed out, which meant the traffic was unlikely to be a problem. He was used to my ways, though, and didn't make an issue of it.

The giant cranes of Harland and Wolff increased in size the closer we came to our destination. My stomach began to somersault. They evoke many memories.

After our goodbyes, I watched until the car disappeared from view. We would have new stories to tell when our lives merged again.

The waiting room of the Isle of Man Steam Packet Company felt cold. Or perhaps, because I was nervous, it only seemed that way. There were few people about when I sat down in the back row of blue upholstered chairs, but it soon began to get busier.

A family of five sat down opposite. Immediately, each member became totally absorbed in their mobile phone. My own phone, a magazine and notebook were on the vacant seat beside me. I was unable to make use of any of them

Many of my fellow travellers were lured to the small hot food bar, in the corner, by the smell of bacon frying. A short time later, they returned to their seats with steaming plates and paper cups. I had no appetite ahead of my third sea crossing to Mona's Isle.

A little girl walked into the room, holding her mother's hand. The sight of the pair triggered a memory. Slowly, everything around me blurred as I became lost in thought. The years rolled away until I was a child of five again, waiting to board the Isle of Man boat. The recollection was bittersweet for more than one reason.

An announcement brought me back to the present with a jolt. *Manannan* was ready for us. While I waited in line, I thought of my trip to the Island in the summer of 2014. A lot had happened since then.

It was during that week on the Isle of Man that I decided to write *Made in Summerland*: the story of my family's involvement in the tragic fire, and the journey that I have been on since I finally confronted my "demon."

Embarkment complete; the passenger door was firmly shut, then we were off. Soon the green coastlines of Antrim and Down gave way to open water as we left Belfast Lough. Soothed by the rolling waves, I allowed my mind to reflect on the months leading up to the book's publication.

After a bad head cold in the winter of 2009, I experienced my first terrifying episode of vertigo. I didn't know what it was, and I thought there was something badly wrong with me. There wasn't – at that time! (Prior to this I thought vertigo was a dizzy feeling when looking down from a great height.) It recurred only twice in the intervening years; but in the first quarter of 2017, I was having an episode almost every week. I put it down to the pressure of the book. I was staring at a screen for hours and getting very little sleep.

One spring day, I was in a local shop with my daughter when I felt the dreaded spinning begin; slowly at first, then gathering speed until everything was a blur. I couldn't move in case I fell. I clutched my daughter's arm for support. After a few minutes, the world around me gradually came into focus again. I walked unsteadily to the checkout, where I still couldn't see well enough to place my shopping on the counter or to pay. My daughter did both. I chatted to the shop assistant as if there was nothing wrong, but my actions must have seemed very strange.

I was on the alert for a couple of days after the embarrassing incident in the supermarket. Although the bouts of vertigo were frightening, my greatest fear was always that they would happen in public. (Just as I dreaded having a panic attack in front of others.) I considered the things that seemed to trigger the spinning sensation, including bright lights, looking down for long periods and turning my head sharply.

It was a ritual with us to have a "carry out" meal on a Thursday evening. It began when the children were small. After doing the weekly shopping with several fractious youngsters, the prospect of putting it all away before the kitchen became serviceable was unappetising. The "chippy" seemed like a good idea, and so a habit was formed.

In April 2017, we went to Dromore, our closest town, to get a few bits and pieces. It was just an ordinary evening. I had been reluctant to leave my laptop and the tricky paragraph that threatened to get the better of me, but I needed a break and some fresh air. With the groceries purchased, tired and hungry, we decided to go to one of the local takeaways instead of driving another eight miles to Banbridge, which we usually did. Robert sat in the car with our dog while I went in. At the last minute, I decided that I didn't want chips myself and placed a telephone order at another shop. I set off to collect it while the rest of the food was being prepared, turning carefully at the counter so as not to set off the vertigo. The manoeuvre meant I didn't see those people in the queue waiting to be served.

When I returned to the car, my husband had his window down and a big smile on his face. "Did, you see Guy?" he asked, before Tyco nudged him out of the way, tongue lolling in excitement because "Mum" was back. Guy, I thought, running through our acquaintances in my head, but there was no Guy! I looked at him in bemusement. "Guy Martin!" he continued. "He was standing behind you!" We are huge fans of the popular road racer and television personality, and Tyco was named in his honour, but I couldn't believe that Guy would be in sleepy Dromore! Robert must be mistaken. "Look!" he almost shouted. "Over there!". Sure enough, it was Guy Martin crossing the town square. Robert said that he had left just after me. The occupants of a car on the opposite side of the road called out to Guy, and he stopped briefly to chat. We longed to speak to him too, but neither of us wanted to encroach on his privacy. Tyco sniffed the brown paper package next to him, appreciatively, confident that there was something inside for him. He pawed the back of the driver's seat, keen to be on the move. Robert turned the key in the ignition, and we set off for home, where Tabitha, our daughter, just in from a long shift, was beside herself when she heard our news!

I resumed work on the book with increased vigour. The experience had brought the Isle of Man close again. A Manx friend had taken great pains to obtain autographs for Tabitha during the TT races. She didn't dare hope that Guy's would be among them, but it was. We were keen to attend the famous races ourselves. For a long time, I couldn't have considered such a busy event, particularly because of the location. It was so nice to think that many things I'd had to say no to in the past, might now be within my grasp. The battle to overcome the effects of the fire in Summerland was hard, and the victories, to some, may have seemed insignificant; but each one was a stepping stone to a future I once feared was out of reach. I truly believed that the worst times of my life were over. I should have known better.

The vertigo didn't return until the latter end of 2018, and then, it was a harbinger of doom

When land appeared again, a young man and his little daughter came to sit in the empty seat in front of mine. The child pointed avidly to things that caught her eye, and her dad responded enthusiastically. I thought of my own father and of how he made long journeys exciting for us. Each one was an adventure. The tenth anniversary of his passing was quickly approaching, but I felt his presence more strongly than ever.

At the sea terminal in Douglas, everyone seemed to have someone to greet them. I knew there were many friends who would have done the same for me; but I needed those moments to compose myself. My reunions with Mona are always emotional.

The taxi driver was familiar, and we chatted easily during the short journey to the Palace Hotel. I savoured each dear familiar landmark: the Victorian Jubilee Clock, the Gaiety Theatre, the Villa Marina and the war memorial on Harris Promenade.

We passed the Empress Hotel, where I first stayed in 2013, with Robert. It was my "home" on the Island many times after that and will always have a special place in my heart.

The majestic Castle Mona, built at the beginning of the nineteenth century for the 4th Duke of Atholl, John Murray, tugged at my heart strings, even though I'd never been inside. Its architect, George Steuart, who arrived from Scotland about ten years before building work began, lived in a lodge on the site now occupied by the Gaiety and the Villa Marina. Stone travelled from the Isle of Arran to be used in the Castle's construction. After the Duke's death and the sale of his estate, Castle Mona became a hotel. It changed hands several times and developed along the way, before closing in 2006.[49] It has been sold now, and I wonder what the future holds. I often stood on the promenade gazing at it, taking in every detail. The words on the plaque above the door, encircling the Three Legs of Mann, are the Island's motto: *Quocunque Jeceris Stabit - Whithersoever you throw it, it will stand*.[50] They are words that gave me great courage when life flung me, mercilessly, in ways from which it seemed, at first, I could never recover.

In my childhood, the sandcastles I built, with such care, had to be a particular shape. I tapped out a tower for the centre of my *castle* from my small sand-filled pail. A scrap of paper on a lollipop stick, saved for that purpose, made a good flag. Perhaps in the recesses of my mind, a memory was stored of a real structure, of a similar shape, in another seaside town – a memory too painful to think about.

We crouched on the beach under clouds full of rain, two little girls with their mummy and daddy. A much-anticipated summer holiday had just begun. Small hands scooped sand into piles, imagination sufficing in the absence of proper equipment – which would be purchased the following day, daddy told us. He always ensured that we had something to look forward to; but it wasn't in his power, on that occasion, to fulfil his promise. Behind us, Castle Mona, so solid and dependable, looked out to sea, sure of its future back then. A longing look was all I could give it on that grey, Thursday evening in Douglas, for we had a date with destiny; and the clock was ticking.

My room at the Palace had a sea view in 2017. When booking each of my previous trips to the Isle of Man, I'd deliberately chosen a room at the back of whichever hotel I would be staying at. Finally, I was ready for the gulls to wake me as they swooped, shrieking on the waves, and to hear the steady rhythm of the trammers plodding to-and-fro. The thought of them stopping at the Terminus, close to the derelict Summerland site, no longer caused me distress. I knew I could see the site from my window, if I chose to, but I could cope with that.

I was conquering my fears, one by one, and I felt empowered.

It was strange to walk along Strand Street and to see *Made in Summerland* in the shop windows – surreal almost. Nicola, from Lily Publications, kindly dropped off some copies at the hotel for my Manx friends, but I realised while I was out that I needed a few more. As the lady in the Lexicon bookshop completed the transaction, I asked her for feedback. Her response brought tears to my eyes.

One of the things I enjoyed most during my stay at the Palace that summer, was coming back to my room and the sound of the sea. I could hear it clearly as I stood in the corridor, searching for the card to unlock the door. I almost expected briny water to gush out when I opened it and thought, regretfully, of all the times that experience could have been mine, if only I had been a little braver.

On my way to breakfast on Monday morning, I glanced into a room which had its door wide open and recalled my first stay at the hotel, the previous year. From my window, then, I could see the houses on Palace Road and beneath them, the leafy cliff and the space where a magnificent pavilion once stood.

The Palace Pavilion Ballroom was the last of the great ballrooms in the capital to open, but it was certainly not the least, as it was reputed to be one of the largest in Europe! Guests could dance from half seven in the evening until eleven on a beautiful oak floor. The forty strong Palace orchestra provided music to accompany acts performing at concerts in the opera house, next door. Both the pavilion and opera house were impeccably decorated, attention to detail was unstinting. Those who undertook the task were among the best in their field. Sadly, less than fifteen years after it opened, the beautiful ballroom suffered fire damage and required extensive reconstruction work. Fire would pay a return visit in 1920.

The pavilion's successor, known as the White Palace – and later the Lido – opened in 1921. It took up a bit more space and was in a more modern style than the pavilion. A theatre built to take over the original function of the opera house, eight years earlier, survived until the mid-sixties, when space was needed for a new hotel. The Palace, also known as the Hilton for a spell, was rising from the ground when architect James Philipps Lomas and assistant architects, Gillinson Barnett and Partners Ltd, were appointed to the Derby Castle redevelopment project. The name Summerland was some way off from being associated with the new entertainment centre, that would come to dominate the northern end of the promenade, when the first guests were welcomed to the Palace Hotel.

The Lido finally closed in 1994, leaving a wealth of memories. All that remains of the Coliseum complex is the opera house, now a cinema. Like the Aquadrome, the opera house escaped the ravages of fire. I intended to visit during one of my stays at the Palace, but it remains on my list of unfulfilled ambitions. Maybe one day![51]

It's difficult to find words to explain what I was feeling when I gazed out at that view. It was as if I was looking at it from someone else's eyes, someone who had looked at it a long time ago. There are many places on the Island which felt familiar when I first saw them. It was as if I knew them already, and they knew me.

On Monday afternoon, I met with local journalist Paul Moulton to do an interview about the book. It was great to see Paul again and to be welcomed into his home. With my usual knack of doing the wrong thing, I had selected a green top to wear that day. Fortunately, I avoided disappearing into the backdrop by having a change of clothes with me! I rarely go on a journey, even a sort one, without a bag full of *essential* items, in case of an emergency! If I didn't, I'd worry that I was tempting fate. I did tempt fate in 2018, and I was punished for it.

Tuesday was glorious. In no time at all, I developed a tan just sitting on the balcony. My skin was much in need of the sun after long months spent indoors. It was wonderful to be able to relax in such a beautiful setting and to be free from worry.

I had intended calling at the Empress Hotel that evening, but tiredness forced me to postpone the visit to my old "home." I slept with the balcony doors open despite being on the fourth floor; my mind was at ease. I didn't fear a sleep-walking incident as I would have done in the past, and dark dreams did not trouble me.

Wednesday, 2nd August 2017 – the forty-fourth anniversary of the fire – arrived, bringing with it memories of that long ago holiday morning. The anniversary flowers, delivered by Clucas florists the previous day, were a cheery sight. As well as the basket for the large memorial in the Kaye Garden, there were two single sunflowers: sunflowers for Summerland – always.

A beautiful service, led by Douglas Borough Council, marked the passing of another year. Her Worshipful the Mayor, Councillor Debbie Pitts, came to chat with me afterwards, and the warmth of her greeting brought tears to my eyes. It was lovely to see all my friends on the council again and to have a catch up.

Before the service, I met a lady whose brother was feared to have been caught up in the tragedy. The family had a very anxious wait until his safety was assured. She accompanied me the short distance to the promenade opposite the Summerland site. It was becoming increasingly difficult for me to go there on the night of the anniversary. I lingered behind when the others, who had been gathered there, were gone.

There was a nip in the air; an early reminder that autumn would soon come knocking, leaving her calling cards scattered on the ground; warning summer that it was on borrowed time!

The last tram of the evening glided by. I crossed the track to the wooden fence in front of the site, where black night enshrouded the empty space. In my hand was a single sunflower. I tucked it into a gap between post and fence. A streetlight shone on the petals making them gleam: a beacon of light and hope for a place that has been in darkness too long.

My day was almost at an end, just one task remained. I turned around and crossed the road to lifebelt twenty-eight.

Chapter 9: Fallen Leaves

But they are gone who used to share
With songs and mirth our joy and care.
Before the Autumn gold was there
They are gone.

(*Autumn Gold* by *Cushag*: Josephine Kermode)

"School days, school days, dear old golden rule days" – words from a book that was a treasured part of my childhood. The book is gone now, and although I've searched for a replacement, I haven't been successful. It was an anthology of wonderful, heart-warming tales, and that particular line appeared in the story of a bear family dressed in human clothes, who illustrate the changing seasons through various activities. Summer and autumn are the seasons I remember best.[52]

In summer, the bears are relaxed, wearing their holiday attire. Baby bear, in his parent's arms, licks a dripping ice-cream. Soon, it is time for his siblings to return to school, where chairs are tucked neatly under desks, awaiting them.

However, in the world beyond the story book, on the first day of the autumn term in 1973, the chair that was to be mine at Newport Primary School, remained unoccupied. There were other empty seats in several schools around Great Britain because their young owners had also gone to Summerland while on holiday. I was fortunate, as I rejoined my class the following year. Nine other children didn't.

***

The giant cranes - Samson and Goliath at Queen's Island in Belfast. (Photo taken by Tabitha Wilson)

I can look at these words without fear now.

The entrance to the magical Summerhill Glen.

The Manx Electric Railway (MER) ticket office.

The statue of Manannan on Binevenagh Mountain. (Photograph taken by Tabitha Wilson)

Summerland memorial in the Kaye Garden.

Mussenden Temple at Downhill. (Photograph taken by Tabitha Wilson)

Scrabo Tower, Newtownards. (Photograph taken by Tabitha Wilson)

One of the beautiful new sunflower seats in the Kaye Garden.

Flowers laid in memory of Eileen Fisher and William Hamilton by my friend Irene Moffat, another Summerland survivor.

My dear companion Tyco.

Sunflowers in bloom in the Kaye Garden, August 2018. (Photograph taken by Maria Darnoult)

The site where Summerland stood. Part of the Aquadrome can be seen, attached to the cliff face. The photo was taken from the footpath behind the Manx Electric Railway sign.

The Sunken Gardens on Loch Promenade, Douglas.

The Kaye Memorial Garden on Queen's Promenade, Douglas. (This lovely photo was taken by Peter Killey, who kindly gave me permission to include it in this book)

The statue of Sir William Hillary at Douglas Head.

Chapter 10: They Come in Threes

I've had some wonderful holidays on the Isle of Man and made many great memories. These days because life has changed so much, and it sometimes feels like I'm drowning, I cling to them with all my might!

Lynne, a lovely member of the Palace housekeeping team, had suggested that I speak to Noel McAteer, manager of the Palace Slots, when I expressed an interest in the history of the hotel. On her recommendation, I went to visit him at his place of work.

When I walked through the door of the "slots," on the last day of July 2017, I felt as if I'd gone back in time. The machines and facilities were modern, but there was an atmosphere so redolent of the 1970's, that I almost gasped. It was a time in my childhood, when, although we had our troubles, there were many special moments too. Memories came tumbling back.

I waited in the café for Noel to arrive for his shift, feeling completely at ease – a sensation I rarely experience – and was lost in thought when he appeared by my side. The Newry Man greeted me warmly, before suggesting that we went into the bingo hall to chat. The music and sounds of the fruit machines faded, when the past entered the room.

Noel was just sixteen when he took up a position as night porter in the popular hotel on Central Promenade. His affable nature endeared him to staff and guests alike. Hard work led to several promotions. Recognition for his years of dedicated service came in the form of several awards, including a trip abroad for Noel and his wife Mary.

Noel described the hotel complex as being "ahead of its time." I'd read that about another centre of entertainment, not far from the Palace. It's an accurate statement in both cases!

Big name groups came to the Island to perform in the Palace Lido, swelling numbers even more. Staff often worked such long hours that when their shifts ended it would be daylight again!

Noel saw many changes over the years. The bingo hall and casino replaced shops and cafés. There was even a bank at one stage. A new "suite," in 1979, marked both change of ownership and the "Manx Millennium"; when the hotel was packed to capacity with people who had travelled to the Isle of Man to take part in the celebrations.

Among the significant events that Noel recalled during an interview, at the time of his retirement – including the occasion when the Bee Gees stayed at the Palace, and everyone was sworn to secrecy – three stood out, as he had also chatted about them with me!

In 1973, Noel was living in rented accommodation on Strathallan Crescent, close to the Aquadrome and Summerland. On the evening of 2nd August, he had gone to work as usual, not expecting anything out of the ordinary to happen; but that would soon change. Flames had been spotted at Summerland.

Noel alerted a manager. Then, he and some of his colleagues got into the hotel minibus and set off immediately. They were unable to get further than the bottom of Summerhill as police were turning traffic away. Instead, they took those people Noel refers to as "the walking wounded," to hospital for treatment. They also gave lifts to members of the public who wanted to donate blood.

The exhausted men had no time to recover because the Palace had become a gathering place for the press; and it was where Summerland staff met, the morning after the fire, for a tragic roll call. Noel referred to the Palace as the "hub" of the Isle of Man, and it became the hub of the fire investigation too. It was unique on the Island in that all the rooms had a telephone, which was essential in that time of crisis. The poignant moment when the centre's young employees discovered that some of their workmates hadn't survived, has stayed with Noel. Some of those who didn't make it were around his age – young men far from home, like him. It was heart-breaking.[63]

About seven months after I was speaking to Noel, I received a message from a Manxman called Geoff. His dad was employed by the Electric Railway company in 1973, and on the night of the fire he was working in the ticket hut, not far from the entertainment complex. Geoff was working too. He drove a taxi for Magee's Radio Cabs every night to make a bit of extra money, which helped with the mortgage. This was in addition to having a fulltime job. Sleep was in short supply. Geoff had to start his main work at 8:00 am, no matter how tired he was.

In the early hours of 3rd August, Geoff was still picking up fares. He stopped on Strathallan Road and looked down on the smoking, warped skeleton of Summerland's solarium. It was a dreadful sight. Geoff sent me some newspaper clippings from an edition of the *Courier*, dated 10th August 1973, which show photographs of the ruined building. They were taken by a holidaymaker who originally came from Co Mayo but was living in Tamworth. The article is captioned, "SUMMERLAND ERUPTS LIKE A VOLCANO." Words that send a shudder down my spine.

Enda O'Donnell's images, which capture the rapid spread of the blaze, were given to the authorities in the hope they would prove useful during the investigation. What started out as "exciting" opportunity for the amateur photographer, turned into a nightmare as he watched a disaster unfold in front of him. The awful truth of the situation dawned on Mr O'Donnell when ambulances arrived at the centre. He was shocked to the core.

That summer was one Geoff would never forget. As well as the fire, another event left an indelible imprint on his mind.

In the early hours of 15th August, the telephone rang and rang in the Golden Egg Restaurant, but no one answered. A lady coming in to clean, some hours later, made a shocking discovery. In the kitchen, surrounded by a pool of blood, was the body of the young manager. The twenty-six-year-old man had arrived on the Island, only a few months before, to take up the position in the premises on Strand Street, which came with lodgings above.

As the investigation into the fire in Summerland was ongoing, a number of CID officers, from Lancashire, remained on the Island. They now had two cases. Other officers, who had just gone home, had to come back again.

Soon, the pieces began to come together, and they were able to establish what had happened.

Geoff was still picking up fares as Tuesday 14th August bled into Wednesday. The new day had barely drawn breath when he was flagged down by fate.

Geoff listened to a story about an ill wife in Newcastle, and the urgency to get back to her. He was sympathetic to the young man's plight, suggesting that he get in touch with the airport or go by boat. Geoff took him to the top of Victoria Street, where the stranger climbed out of Geoff's cab, but not out of his life.

James Richard Lunney, who had the appearance of having exerted himself, went back to his hotel. He had taken a room there, a few hours before, as he had nowhere else to stay. The landlady had evicted him from his lodgings that morning, due to non-payment. Things weren't going well for him.

Another taxi driver was passing the Palace Hotel, around 6:00 am. The street was empty, but he heard whistling and a shout from somewhere above. A man was trying to get his attention from the balcony of a first-floor bedroom. On the way to the airport, the tale was told, again, of a sick relative and the necessity for a speedy return home. He also heard about a successful evening in the casino. When they arrived at Ronaldsway, which was not yet open, no help was needed with the luggage, a single attaché case.

The early arrival was advantageous for the traveller. A flight to Blackpool was arranged with the aid of an officer in the airport police force. In an act of kindness, the policeman had contacted a pilot, who was willing to accommodate Lunney, and while waiting for him to arrive provided coffee and company. Soon the pilot and his passenger were taking off in a two-seater plane.

There was no ill relative on the adjacent isle. When the body of Nigel Neal was discovered at the Golden Egg restaurant, the plane carrying the person responsible for the crime was touching down on English soil; ready for the next stage of his attempt to evade prosecution.

The perpetrator was finally tracked down in Edinburgh. Geoff was among a number of people who gave evidence at the trial in Douglas, later in the year. More than four decades had passed since the last murder trial on the Isle of Man. It was heard in front of Deemster Robert Eason. When I discovered this, I couldn't help thinking back to the occasion I appeared in front of the eminent briw. In my case, this occurred in his private chambers. Nonetheless, beforehand, due to my tendency to catastrophise, I imagined something bad was going to happen to me. I was nine; old enough to understand many things and to misunderstand even more. I'd watched judges in television programmes place a black cap on their head and pronounce a sentence of execution. I felt that in some way I was responsible for the fire in Summerland, because of an incident in our boarding house, and that maybe the deemster would place the cap on his head in my presence! I needn't have worried; the sleepless nights were unfounded. Deemster Eason was very kind and put me at my ease. He reminded me of one of my uncles; and I felt foolish afterwards for having worried so much!

Five years before I met him, Robert Eason passed a sentence of death, by hanging, upon the man responsible for "The Golden Egg Murder," on receipt of a unanimous (as required under Manx law) decision by the twelve jurors. (The murder weapon, discovered two days after the crime, was a fire extinguisher.) He did not don a black cap then, nor was the guilty man executed. The actual punishment for killing Mr Neal, who left a young wife and two small children, was life imprisonment. I wonder if this knowledge would have made me more, or less nervous, before I met Deemster Eason![64]

Noel McAteer had completed check-in for a young man in the early hours of 15th August. The man provided an answer to the unasked question about his lateness, by explaining that he was a pilot who had had to make a "forced landing!" Noel, courteous and helpful as always, fetched a shirt and tie for him to wear, to enable him to enter the casino. He had no idea, then, that he had met the "Golden Egg murderer!"

The third event Noel spoke of, occurred a week before the murder trial began.

Noel was on his way to work, when he realised there was a fire at the Palace Hotel. It was hard to believe, coming as it did, just a few months after the tragedy at Summerland. Many bedrooms were destroyed including that of the chairman of the Summerland fire commission, who was staying at the hotel for the course of the Inquiry. Thankfully, there were no casualties. A calm and extremely organised evacuation ensured the safety of staff and guests.

Since August, stories had been circulating about acts of heroism: lives saved because of the bravery of others. Another young porter at the hotel had been very impressed by what he heard, and he wanted to be a hero too! He had a plan! A fire was started in the dining room extension using methylated spirits from the kitchen. Once given life, the fire at the Palace grew quickly. It chose its own path – up and over the balconies and into the bedrooms. A set of fire doors finally put a stop to its gallop. The would-be hero must have been horrified by the result of his actions. He had wanted to be the one who alerted everyone to the danger lurking in the dining room, to be seen bringing people to safety. Instead, his scheme had gone awry, and the cost to human life could have been devastating.

One young man who genuinely had the wellbeing of others at heart, was Noel's brother Hughie. His actions were not premeditated. As soon as word reached the Crescent, where Hughie was employed as a barman, he rushed straight to Summerland. He was familiar with the exits and a number of those fleeing the inferno ran to him for help, believing him to be an employee, (Hughie was wearing a white jacket and a dickie bow, the uniform of many bar staff at the time), and the brave young man was able to lead many people to safety.

It takes a very special kind of person to put the safety of others before their own…

Chapter 11: No Greater Love

When faced with danger, our sense of self-preservation almost always kicks in. Adrenalin courses through our veins preparing us for flight. For some people in Summerland, when fire roared through the building, flight was not their immediate thought. Those individuals decided to fight; they fought for the lives of others. They fought for people they knew and also for people who were strangers to them; people they might never see again and who, on the most part, would never discover the identity of the person who risked his or her own life to save theirs. They did not think of themselves as heroes, but that is exactly what they are!

Little Robert Timmins was enjoying himself on the *Astroglide*, when a man ran by shouting about a fire!

Rather than rush for an emergency exit, in panic, as others were doing, the Girvan lad got off the slide and calmly brought an eleven-year-old girl to safety, then returned to the burning building to rescue her brother. As this point, flames were sweeping down the stairs to the children's entertainment levels, and hot ash was dropping from the roof. Robert made his way to where a little boy was still playing, oblivious to his perilous position. Soon, four-year-old Gary was reunited with his sister Lisa, to their father's huge relief. Sometime after they returned to Northern Ireland, he wrote to Mr and Mrs Timmins expressing gratitude for their son's courage and inviting him to their home.

Robert was the only member of his family in the complex when fire broke out. His parents, Frank (a lorry driver) and Margaret, and his sisters, Anne aged eleven and Sandra, eight (sadly Anne has now passed away) decided to go to somewhere else instead. They had visited Summerland every night since they arrived on the Island the week before. Robert, at the age of twelve, was considered responsible enough to spend time in the entertainment centre – his "favourite" place – alone. This, he proved beyond measure. He truly is one of the heroes of the Summerland tragedy.

Robert's sister recently came across a weekly ticket from that memorable holiday. It gave a child unlimited access to all the facilities in Summerland, apart from the disco and Sundome. Ticket number 3750 cost sixty pence and expired on 3rd August 1973![65]

A sixteen-year-old youth, who was employed on the roller-skating rink, did not flee for his life without thinking of others. He forced open doors to allow terrified youngsters to escape, and his bravery has never been forgotten by Frank Keenan, who had been his colleague in a local factory before he left to take up the position in Summerland.[66]

Johnny Silver – DJ in the underground disco – was an undoubtable hero. After rescuing at least two hundred youngsters, he faced the inferno again and helped many more terrified people to escape. In the aftermath of the tragedy he was seen walking with the aid of a stick. This was due to an injury he sustained when breaking the fall of a toddler who had been thrown from a balcony.

Pauline Wynne-Smythe, wearing sunglasses, to soothe her aching eyes, drew in grateful breaths of fresh air while she walked with her husband and little boys in Port St Mary on a lovely sunny day. The "shy" lady felt unable to speak about her terrifying ordeal.

Mrs Wynne-Smythe had been the manageress of the Marquee Showbar. Her diligence and quick-thinking saved many lives. She was unusual among Summerland staff in that she had some training in fire safety and had read a notice in the bar's office about evacuation.

Ken Harding, the technical services manager, battled the kiosk fire with a hand-held extinguisher until it became clear that it was out of control. He had the presence of mind to turn off the upward moving escalator, as people were struggling to get down and unlocked an emergency exit as well.

Mr Harding had previously read a document in the control room about procedure in an emergency. He gave Pauline the order to evacuate, and she immediately sprang into action.[67] Time was not on her side. The task to empty the room of more than two hundred occupants was not an easy one. The sense of urgency didn't seem to penetrate the consciousness of some, and they wanted to delay their escape by gathering up belongings or waiting for change. The courageous manageress directed people to the emergency staircase on the north-east side, thus avoiding the congested flying staircase, where most of those on the upper floors fled because it was familiar to them. It wasn't until the bar was empty, that Pauline made her own way out. This was not without great difficulty due to the fire's rapid spread.

Mrs Wynne-Smythe spent several days in hospital as the heat and toxic smoke had almost blinded her. Thankfully her sight improved, and she was once again able to enjoy life with her precious sons, who were aged between ten months and ten years. The trauma of that terrible night was always in the background, however, and she suffered from nightmares. Her family were her constant support.[68]

Sadly, Mrs Wynne-Smythe, whose heroism during the Summerland fire will never be forgotten, passed away in 2009.

Allan Williams, thirty-seven, suffered an horrific ordeal in Summerland. The bereaved father was still in Whiston Hospital in November 1973. He and his eldest son, Allan junior, thirteen, found themselves trapped on the flying staircase when the family of five became separated. Like my father, they had decided to leave when they saw smoke, despite the compere's advice not to panic.

Mr Williams, who described the entertainment centre as "a great place" for children, threw his son over the railings in desperation. The lad dropped some thirty feet without mishap. Unfortunately, his father, when attempting to jump from the same place, caught his foot between the bars. Suspended upside down, with his clothes alight, the car worker struggled to free himself. Managing to jack-knife his body, he released his foot and dropped to the floor. The shocked man, who was still on fire, suddenly realised that his son was next to him. Young Allan hadn't tried to get out. He had refused to leave his father. With his bare hands he extinguished the flames, then the pair – Mr Williams aided by Allan – made their way to a door that was open. They were reunited with Mrs Williams and Dawn, who ran towards them open armed.

Allan Williams, when speaking from his hospital bed, said he was hopeful of being discharged before Christmas. Though, it would have been a very sad Christmas for the family without eleven-year-old-Gary. There is a particular word to describe the actions of Mr Williams' eldest son on that tragic night: "heroic."[69]

Sally Naden, a dancer in Summerland, recalls band members carrying a table to the huge window between the Solarium and the Aquadrome. It was their only way out, and as they battered the plate glass as hard as they could, it seemed that it wasn't going to break. The heat was intensifying by the second. Eventually, it yielded to the force, and the dancers and band made their escape through the shattered glass.[70]

"She was marvellous," said one of the guests at the Ravensdale Hotel, on Strathallan Crescent, of Doreen Jackson.

The Douglas landlady had been told by her guests that they had seen black smoke issuing from Summerland. She immediately ran outside to look. By then, the smoke had been joined by flames. It was around twenty minutes to eight. After making a call to emergency services, the landlady hurried the short distance to the blazing building. She was met with a shocking sight.

A man collapsed onto the ground where Miss Jackson was standing. Bystanders explained how he had burst open two doors close to the entrance to let people out, including terrified children. Overcome by his efforts, and probably by the smoke he'd inhaled, he lay unconscious. Doreen and a doctor, who had just arrived at the scene, carried the man to a police car. Then they discovered a lady whose hair had been burned off the back of her head. Her clothes were charred too. They lifted the dazed woman into the same car.

The pair returned to the pandemonium that now existed outside Summerland, to see who else they could help. Panicked people were climbing over one another to escape, and some of those who had made it out realised their children weren't there and were desperately trying to get back in.

Doreen explained how there were several explosions, the first of which was extremely loud. She watched as the front wall "went up in a column of flame," and "debris rained down" on them.

Some people believed, at that time, that the fire had started in one of the machines in the amusement arcade. They spoke of the failure to put it out with a fire-extinguisher.

Miss Jackson returned to her hotel to look after the wounded people who had been brought there; and to comfort those in great distress because of what they'd just experienced.

"I don't know what they would have done without her," said one of Miss Jackson's guests.[71]

Richard Davis, an author, was a young policeman in 1973. It had been his duty to take news of the blaze to the Superintendent, who was at a function, before driving to Summerland. Once there, Richard entered the building through a door at the east side, away from the direction the flames were travelling in. Although he had no breathing apparatus, he worked alongside the firemen in very difficult circumstances. Their task was both sad and distressing.

Having never been in Summerland before, Richard had no idea of the layout of the smoke-filled building. During an interview, a few years ago, he made a very good point. He felt that it would have been advantageous if the emergency services had visited Summerland (and other large buildings), to familiarise themselves with the interior.

Richard had not been given orders to enter the burning complex, but he chose to go in to do what he could, risking his life in the process.[72]

Mike Ventre, who passed away in 2010 at the age of seventy-nine, was affectionately referred to as "The grandfather of the fire service in the Isle of Man."

Mike, who had been keen to learn a trade, started his working life as a painter and decorator. Following a spell of National Service as a Royal Marine Commando, which he thoroughly enjoyed, he felt that it was time for a career change.

After nine months as an auxiliary firefighter with the Borough of Douglas Fire Brigade, Mike took up a full-time position.

Over the years, Mike saw big changes – modernisations and the service being "taken over" by the Isle of Man Government. He recalled several fires that stood out. Some even had a touch of humour attached. When the subject of Summerland was raised, he referred to it as "a nasty business." He was sad that his colleagues, who worked tirelessly that night, received no commendation. Mike felt that if it hadn't been for those firemen, the death toll may have been considerably higher!

"Some of those lads worked themselves to death on that," said Mike.

Mike's devotion to the Isle of Man fire service and his input, which contributed to its progression over the years, were rewarded in 2007. Accompanied by his daughter Maria and the Island's chief and deputy chief fire officers: Brian Draper and Bruce Kirkham, he travelled to Cambridge to attend the annual Spirit of Fire award ceremony. This event was arranged by the Fire Services National Benevolent Fund, an organisation Mike dedicated himself to following his retirement. He had no idea until his name was announced that he had been nominated for an award – the most prestigious of the evening. The Lifetime Achievement Award was presented by Michael Aspel. It was "well-deserved," said Mr Draper, when he expressed his delight, and that of the fire community on the Isle of Man, that Mr Ventre's endeavours had been recognised in this way.[73]

Mike Ventre was not the only one to remark on the lack of acknowledgment of what the firemen did that night. A Douglas doctor described their behaviour as "incredible" and above and beyond their duty. He spoke of how they went into Summerland over and over to rescue people. Not for a second did they hesitate, he said, though the heat was "intense."

This man, who was there from the very start, saw staff battling the fire on the terrace with extinguishers. He thought it was a minor incident until flames shot up the front wall. The emergency services began to arrive. He watched firemen and police officers enter the building through what he believed to be a staff entrance, opposite the Manx Electric Railway sheds. Their task could not have been more difficult. Summerland was in darkness.

The doctor highlighted the criticism, that he felt was directed towards the Island, in the wake of the disaster, and the lack of acknowledgement regarding the magnificent response of the emergency services to such a challenging situation. He recalled the "tremendous" job done by the Police and Fire Services, Noble's Hospital, the St John's Ambulance Service and the Civil Defence, among others. I remember someone telling me about Green Goddesses attending the scene.

"I don't think justice has been done," said the gentleman, who also believed there were significantly fewer casualties because of the courage shown by firemen. The doctor made his feelings clear to Cyril Pearson, the Island's chief fire officer. I agree with him completely, those men deserve the highest commendation. Perhaps it is not too late to do something about it![74]

[On 7th December 1973, the *Isle of Man Examiner* reported that Cyril Pearson had been made a *Fellow of the Institution of Fire Engineers*, a few months before; one of the first in the British Isles to receive the honour.]

Former chief fire officer, Alan Christian, believes that the outcome at Summerland may have been very different if the fire brigade had been called some twenty minutes earlier. There were fire alarm points throughout the building, any one of which, if triggered, would have alerted the station immediately, and help would soon have been on the way.

Doctor Richard Hamm, a GP, did not drive his car to Summerland. The brave man broke a window and lowered himself into the flaming Solarium. Dr Hamm assisted firemen to carry out those overcome by smoke. Alan Christian was the driver of the first engine to arrive at the catastrophic scene. He had a resuscitator on his vehicle and, together with Dr Hamm, worked, next to one of the fire exits, to revive those overcome by smoke. It was exhausting, but they didn't flag.[75]

Dr Hamm, a reluctant hero, when pushed, and with reticence, said that as far as he was aware no one left where he was "without a pulse." To him, his actions weren't in the least courageous. "It's a fact of life…if you can help, you help."

Countless lives were saved because of these brave men. Both heroes of that tragic night.[76]

None of the firemen, who attended the blaze at Summerland, had seen anything like it before. They weren't expecting to be confronted by an inferno when they responded to the call. As retired firefighter, John Skinner, explained, there had been several cases of the automatic alarm going off in the complex, without there actually being a fire, so they were not prepared for the terrifying sight that was revealed when they turned onto the promenade.

When John woke up on 2nd August 1973, he remembered, with excitement, that it was the day he was collecting his wife and new-born son from the maternity home to begin their life as a little family of three. The happiness of John's first day of leave was shattered when the fire bell rang in his house, shortly after 8:00 pm. He set off for the station immediately.

Two appliances had left already, and John was on the third engine, which had the turn-table ladder. All kinds of thoughts must have been flooding the men's minds as they approached the dreadful scene; but on arrival, they were completely focused on the perilous task ahead.

Distraught people were pouring out of Summerland in their thousands as John made his way in. The air was filled with screams. By then, the Oroglas panels had gone and only what John describes as the "residue," was burning. I remember flames chasing each other around the edges of the empty frames, when Mum and I were making our escape. The acrylic panels didn't soften and fall from their frames as the architect believed they would. Instead, the Oroglas ignited and dripped onto the people below. The commission investigating the fire made important recommendations regarding the use of plastic materials in construction, which I hoped, when I read the report in 2014, had been heeded.[77]

John didn't make it home that evening to support his wife during their first night with baby Richard. He was sent into the Aquadrome to pump water from the pool. Using five portable pumps, which were topped up with petrol brought by a colleague, when checking to see if he was ok, John emptied the pool by morning. It was Monday before his holiday began.

I only discovered recently that John had listened to the BBC Radio Four documentary *The Summerland Story*, which was broadcast in August 2012. After an interview in front of the derelict site, on that poignant trip, I was taken to the Kaye Memorial Garden, where I saw the commemorative plaque for the first time. John took to heart what I said there.

In the autumn of 2012, John, a member of Douglas Borough Council, put forward a proposal to the Leader of the council. He agreed. The following May, I discovered there would be a new memorial for the 40th anniversary of the fire. It would have the names of the fifty men women and children who lost their lives engraved on it. I can't begin to describe how emotional that moment was.

John was elected Mayor of Douglas in 2016. We had a lovely chat after the service in the Kaye Garden on the anniversary, and he introduced me to the Mayoress, his wonderful wife Gill. We became firm friends. During my dark time, two years later, a letter from Gill gave me strength at my lowest ebb. It is an absolute honour to have the friendship of this very special couple, and I can never thank them enough for their kindness and support.[78]

Stanley Wyllie Kellet, from Falkirk, had been enjoying the cabaret when Summerland went on fire. The Isle of Man was a break from the Kellet's traditional Scottish holiday destination. Stan's sister and her son David, thirteen, had accompanied Stan, his wife Betty and their two children to the Island. Margaret had become a widow a short while before.

Stan got his family out safely but returned to the building. When his name appeared on the missing list, a close relation knew immediately what had happened. He was a brave and selfless individual. Stanley Kellet, who had been employed by the Electricity Board, lost his life trying to save others. He was thirty-seven years old.[79]

Twenty-three-year-old bar manager, Keith Maceachern, did not flee for his life when disaster befell his place of employment. The safety of others was paramount to him. When he returned to the blazing building for a third time to look for staff members, he didn't make it out. Keith, who should have had decades of life ahead of him, and who had a baby on the way, made the ultimate sacrifice.

It was the evening of 2nd August 1973, and fifteen-year-old Christine Carr was full of excitement. It was just over a week until her cousin Alan's twenty-first birthday. He would be returning from his summer job on the Isle of Man to celebrate the special event, which was to take place in a local hotel. Chris, who had a new dress for the occasion, as did her sister, was looking forward to seeing Alan. They were a close family. Alan was the only child of her mother's sister, and he had been looked after by his aunt when he was little.

At 10:00 pm, the music coming from the television announced the beginning of the news. Chris and her family gathered around the set. What they saw there changed everything.

Alan Barker had such a promising future. At just twenty years old, the young civil servant worked in the fingerprints department of Scotland Yard, had dreams of owning his own bar one day, and the potential to play football professionally. While waiting for a transfer from London, closer to home, he decided to find some holiday work because he found living in the capital expensive. A big entertainment complex on the Isle of Man was hiring. Alan was offered a job and was soon on his way to Douglas with his friend Sean Kelly, twenty-one, who had moved to London with him. They would both be working in bars in Summerland.

The move to the peaceful island in the Irish Sea was a huge relief for Alan's parents. He was their only son and they worried about him. While in London, Alan narrowly escaped being caught up in an IRA bomb. He left a pub just minutes before an explosion occurred. Mr and Mrs Barker received a call from their son, almost straightaway, to let them know he was safe. That call did not come on 2nd August, when they discovered that Summerland was on fire.

Chris remembers how anxious she felt while she watched updates on television, scarcely able to breathe. A policeman brought the news they had been dreading. It seemed incomprehensible to Alan's family that they would never see his big smile again. When a manager from Summerland telephoned Ernest Barker and told him that his son saved the lives of seventeen people, it was some consolation. "That was the lad we had brought up, and it made us proud," he said.

"You couldn't meet a nicer man," than Mr Barker, Chris told me. He was a tremendous support to his wife Doris (known as Dot) – who continued to talk about their son in the present tense – while struggling with his own grief.

Alan, after leading others to safety, became trapped in the blazing building. The staircase, where he had helped others to make their escape, was burnt through. He and a colleague, Graham Harding, took refuge in a storeroom. They drenched themselves with water from a nearby sink, and Graham held his coat over them both. When rescuers found them, sometime later, Graham, though suffering the effects of toxic fumes, was still alive. Alan was gone.

Sean Kelly, from Woolston, did not survive the tragedy either. A few years ago, I had a chat with someone who knew Sean and remembered him and Alan setting off for the Isle of Man. He spoke of Sean's enthusiasm and bright smile and recalled hearing the dreadful news about the young friends.

John McGinty played football with Alan and Sean when they were all members of the Church Street Labour Club. Alan won many trophies for football in his lifetime, and his cousin Chris believes a trophy may have been named in his honour after his passing.

Not a day goes by when John doesn't think of his friends: Alan with his amiable personality and "smile that could light up a room," and Sean, the "character of the group." Life was never dull in Sean's company. Both lads had hearts of gold.

Alan's funeral took place on 9th August, in Warrington Parish Church, where he had been christened when he was a month old. It was attended by colleagues from Scotland Yard. Many tributes were paid to the popular young man, buried on the day before what would have been his twenty-first birthday.

The pain of losing Alan is still as sharp for Chris, her younger sister Jeanette and their mum Win. Time has not dulled the ache. When Jeanette's son was born, she asked her Uncle Ernie and Aunty Dot to be his Godparents. It was a poignant moment when the little boy received his name. He was called Alan, in honour of his brave cousin who gave up his life for others – a true hero of the Summerland fire disaster.[80]

Chapter 12: See a Pin

Eileen Ritchie and her fiancé William Hamilton were walking along Douglas promenade when Eileen spotted a safety pin lying on the ground in front of them. Superstition made her stoop down to pick it up.

The young couple were looking forward to an evening in Summerland, having heard a lot about it from other guests in their hotel. Eileen said the conversation at breakfast that morning had been full of praise for the entertainment centre, and they were keen to see it for themselves.

Twenty-two-year-year old Eileen, from Comber, and Will, from Newtownards, who was several years older, had arranged their trip after Eileen's parents arrived back from a wonderful holiday on the Isle of Man. They even booked the same place to stay.

The time before the fire became blurred for Eileen as the years passed. However, she remembered being on one of the upper terraces when the announcement about a "chip fire" was made. They listened to advice not to panic, but just a short time later pandemonium broke out.

Flames seemed to appear from nowhere. Eileen and Will made their way to the railings at the edge of the balcony. Eileen believed that Will may have pushed her over them, and out of the path of the fire, because she was too frightened to make the leap herself. A canopy broke her fall, saving her from further injury. Eileen sustained burns to her lower back, hands and one of her feet. She also had a minor burn at the side of her eye, which thankfully didn't leave a scar. Like many others, who had also been burnt, Eileen wasn't aware of the extent of her injuries until later. Adrenalin drove her on. After being shoved through a broken window by another fleeing person, Eileen's next memory was of being helped over a high "wall" by a kind stranger.

The "wall" was, in fact, a fence at the end of the outdoor terrace, close to the building's main entrance. Although it was some three feet tall on the crazy golf side, the total drop to the next level was six feet or more. Climbing it may not have been a challenge for the young and agile, but would have proved very difficult, if not impossible, without assistance, for some older people and the injured. An elderly lady from Ramsey was one of the former.

Mrs Kneale had gone into Summerland, around 7:30 pm, as one of a party of five. With her were three members of her family: daughter Dorothy, son-in-law Robert and granddaughter Diane. The fifth person was her lodger Mr Eddie Mudie.

A discussion had taken place earlier about what they might do on that wet Thursday evening. Summerland, when put forward as a possible venue, seemed ideal. The Summerland Story advertising brochure referred to the centre as the "biggest entertainment complex under one roof in the world." Mr Mudie, former labourer on a farm in Glen Auldyn, hadn't yet visited the climate-controlled building and readily accepted an invitation to join the others.

The seventy-six-year-old lady explained to the Isle of Man Examiner that Dorothy had spotted smoke coming from the ceiling when they were in the vicinity of the slot machines. More smoke became visible. Mrs Kneale was informed that it appeared to be only a corner of the building that was affected, and the situation was "under control," but this turned out not to be the case. A member of staff, carrying a walkie-talkie, was urging people to hurry.

With flames just yards behind them, and heeding advice about which direction to go, they managed to get out. On the terrace, Mrs Kneale was assisted over the fence by Robert and another man. The elderly lady believed that at one point she may have been upside down, clinging on, unable to get a foothold because of the closely linked wire. Finally, on solid ground again, shaken by her ordeal, Mrs Kneale, along with Dorothy and Robert, made it to safety via the concrete staircase that led to the car park. There, they were reunited with Diane and Eddie, who had been separated from them in the panic. A huge explosion shook the already trembling survivors further.

Mrs Kneale, widow of Mooragh Park's one-time head gardener, felt they were incredibly fortunate to have escaped due to the rapid development of the fire.[81]

Luck was not on the side of William Robert Hamilton, known to his family as Wilbert. To Eileen, he was Will. After pushing Eileen to safety, he had been unable to save himself.

The Hamiltons lived on Scrabo Road, a few miles from Newtownards in Co Down; and when I discovered this, memories of childhood trips to the landmark watchtower on the hill came flooding back. Aching legs from the climb were soon forgotten when the view spread out before us.

Scrabo Tower, a nineteenth century folly – memorial to the 3rd Marquess of Londonderry: Charles Vane – was originally known as the Londonderry Monument. The late gentleman's eldest son and his second wife, London-born, Frances Anne Vane – the Marquess changed his surname from his birthname Stewart to Vane, upon his marriage – decided to build a monument in his honour. (However, the pair may have had conflicting opinions. A monument was also built in Durham, as the Marquess had resided for the most part in England when he married again.) Money for the local project was raised by local people of similar status, friends of the late Marquess and some tenants.

Scrabo Hill was chosen because of the accessibility of stone for its construction and because it would be visible from Mount Stewart, the seat of the Marquis of Londonderry. Building work began in 1857 and ended two years later when funds were depleted. It wasn't as high as originally intended and perhaps not as elaborate, but a spectacular sight, nonetheless.[82]

Mr and Mrs Ritchie travelled to the Isle of Man as soon as they discovered that the young couple had been caught up in the disaster.

Their daughter's first words to them were, "Where's Will?" Eileen said she felt reassured when they told her that he was in a different hospital. Some of the injured had been flown to Liverpool, and she believed him to be there. It was considered that the truth would be detrimental to the young woman, given her vulnerable state.

Eileen was flown back to Northern Ireland for further treatment and to face a future without Will. She clearly remembers the ambulance journey and the realisation that she wasn't being taken home as she first thought.

Eileen was initially kept in isolation in the Ulster Hospital, Dundonald, to prevent her burns from becoming infected, as were mum and I. Desperate for a cigarette, to relieve her anxiety, Eileen asked her mother to hold one to her lips because her hands were encased in dressings.

The friendship between my parents and the Ritchies, which began in Dundonald, continued after our discharge. Although I was just six years old, I remember the visit to Eileen's home in Comber. Mr Ritchie began to talk about the fire and Eileen recalled that my father said, "Not in front of the children," and we were sent upstairs with her. Eileen, who needed to get ready for a night out, wasn't happy with the arrangement. She laughed when she told me about chasing us from her room so she would have peace to put on her make-up! I laughed too. Lynda, I know, would have had a keen interest in the lipstick and other items on the dressing table, and I am certain that I would have been asking lots of questions!

At the time of the fire, Eileen was a switchboard operator for Tennants Textile Colours Limited, a company which made dyes for other companies all over the world. She enjoyed her job and returned to work when sufficiently recovered; however, Eileen had to stop work again after just a few years because of issues with her health.

Eileen and Will met in the square in Newtownards, where many young people gathered to sit in cars, chatting and joking. It reminds me of my teenage years, when Lisburn car park was the place to be.

It was a momentous occasion when a young person drove there for the first time after passing their test! I did the same; and proudly manoeuvred my second-hand red Ford Fiesta into a parking space next to a friend, who had recently passed her test too. I wish I'd had the courage to persevere with driving, but my fear of an accident, and the vehicle becoming engulfed in flames, was too strong to overcome.

As often happens with friendships over time, we lost touch with the Ritchies. After an article about Summerland was published in the *Belfast Telegraph*, in 2016, journalist, Claire McNeilly contacted me with exciting news! She had the telephone number of a lady who had also been in the fire. Lack of response to a similar article, the previous year, had left me feeling despondent. I had been so hopeful, then, that someone from Northern Ireland would contact me to share their memories of the tragedy.

It was a sunny late spring afternoon, when I called Eileen. I was so nervous, though I needn't have worried. We were soon chatting like old friends. We discovered lots of things in common. We both loved animals, reading and spicy food! Eileen explained that she had married her childhood friend, George, and sadly lost him after he suffered a heart attack. We talked for ages. I couldn't wait to tell Mum that I'd been speaking to Eileen. Mr Ritchie had kept newspaper cuttings about the fire, and she was keen to show them to us.

Eileen was troubled with her back, which meant she was often housebound. Prior to this, she was "always on the go." Eileen enjoyed many holidays, often to Spain, but Summerland was never far from her mind. She checked for fire exits and sat near a door when she was out, just as I do!

Unfortunately, as well as the ongoing trouble with her back, Eileen developed leukaemia. She was saddened to learn of my father's passing and interested to discover that he, too, had a blood-related cancer. In his case, it was multiple myeloma.

Eileen never gave up hope that she would recover sufficiently to visit the Kaye Garden. She longed to see Will's name on the beautiful memorial. We planned to go together and often chatted about it; but Eileen's dearest wish would never be granted.

A memorial stands on Scrabo Hill, commemorating the life of a gentleman who was cherished by his family and friends; though for me, the monument calls to mind a loving and much-loved couple whose desire to spend time on the magical Isle of Man ended in tragedy.

***

[In November, last year, Eileen's dear friend, Ruth, contacted me with the sad news that Eileen had passed away. Her telephone calls had gradually become less frequent. There was no answer when I rang her. She had been sleeping a lot, and I think I knew, deep down, that the end was coming.

Eileen, thank you for the years we had. You raised my spirits when I was feeling low, and I hope I did the same for you. Our sense of humour, so similar, got us through the hard times. How I loved to hear your voice when I answered the phone and the question you asked every time: "When are we going for that curry?"]

Chapter 13: From Generation unto Generation

The year seven class at Onchan Primary School was given an assignment: an end of term project. Luke Corkish, aged eleven, chose the Summerland fire. I think I would have cheered if I had been there when he made his decision.

✳✳✳

Young David Corkish, with his father and sister, had watched in horror as Summerland became engulfed in flames.

On Thursday 2nd August 1973, David and his sister were looking forward to a visit to the entertainment centre. However, the milking on their family farm was late finishing, and by the time they were finally on their way black smoke was rising into the sky. If work on the farm had finished on schedule, the Corkish family may well have been inside the complex when disaster struck. That thought is never far from David's mind.

David told his son Luke, a keen young farmer with a great passion for New Holland tractors, and his daughter Kirree about the fire on many occasions. When driving past the derelict site, he explained that he had never forgotten those flames! These recollections, along with the fact that the tragedy is an important part of the Island's history, prompted Luke to write about Summerland

I first met Luke in 2014, on the 41st anniversary, when he came along to a service on the promenade with his dad and sister (he also attended the unveiling of the new memorial the previous year). I had been chatting to David about Summerland on Facebook, and it was lovely to speak to him in person and to be introduced to his family.

I was really looking forward to seeing Luke's project, but it was out on loan. When I visited the Island again, a few months later, I arranged to meet him and his dad for lunch. As we took our seats in the Terminus Tavern on Strathallan Crescent, I thought about my first visit, almost two and a half years earlier. That day had a feeling of unreality. If someone had told me, then, that I would return to the Island alone and enjoy a relaxed lunch with Manx friends, close to the place that changed my life, I would not have believed them. In May 2012, I could barely swallow the food. My kindly companions insisted that I had something to eat before my flight home, but I was overwrought. The weeks leading up to the trip were filled with worry as my mind presented one horrifying scenario after the other; but I didn't give in. I had to go back. A fear of flying, coupled with the terror of revisiting the scene of my nightmares pushed me to my limits. It was wonderful, therefore, to be back at the Terminus in completely different circumstances.

Reading what Luke had written and chatting to him about how the fire affected me, was extremely moving.

When it was time to hand in his project, Luke had placed it on a table in the hallway at school, along with the others, where it could be viewed by visitors. "A lot of people saw it and stood at the table wanting to know more about it," said Luke, who continued his education, post-primary, at St Ninian's High School. "Some remember seeing the flames," he added.

I'm so proud to know this empathetic young man. I grew up believing that few people remembered or cared about us – the victims of the Summerland fire. I worried that new generations would be unaware of the disaster. Luke's words give me so much hope.

"People need to remember the past in order for the future to be different, with lessons being learnt to stop such a tragic event ever happening again."

I met James Drew Turner in August 2016, on the evening of the 43rd anniversary of the fire. He was taking photos for a project that would form part of his degree. We chatted on the promenade opposite the Summerland site, where I had gone to pay my respects to the memories of that awful night. A concrete bridge once spanned the King Edward Road, and we stood close to the spot on which it had discharged distraught men, women and children who'd escaped the inferno.

It was a wet night and daylight was dwindling rapidly. I wanted to visit the Kaye Garden before returning to my hotel. Jamie came with me, and it was nice to have company and to continue our chat.

We glanced at the memorial plaque as we entered that special place. The words are familiar to me, as I've read them many times.

The garden commemorates former mayor and mayoress of Douglas, Joseph and Sarah Jane Kaye (1904 – 1905), whose son, Sydney, made a bequest to the council. Work was finished in 1955.

Joseph Kaye JP was eighty-two when he passed away. Ill health had plagued him for a while, but he rose above his trials and continued to work for the benefit of the people of Douglas in whatever capacity he could. Mr Kaye was held in high esteem in all aspects of his life.

In the 1860s, Joseph Kaye exchanged hair wax for candle wax when he left his hairdressing business on Duke Street, to become a chandler, taking up the reins in his father's factory. Three decades later, it was time for him to quit the Lord Street premises for a new venture. He made a success of everything he turned his hand to, and his new position as a director of the Douglas Gas Light Company was no exception. He became chairman of the board after ten years. Even when he retired, on health grounds, his opinion was much sought after and valued.

Mr Kaye was elected to the council in 1894. It was an exciting time for Douglas, as many changes were taking place in the capital during the last few decades of the old century and the early years of the new. Joseph Kaye was very much part of it all. How fitting that the garden, named in his honour, is home to the statue of Sir Hall Caine. Caine also witnessed the developments in the capital and the influx of tourists that followed. The names of both men are linked with the Steam Packet Company. Alderman Kaye served as chairman in its heyday.

The death occurred of that eminent citizen less than a year after the end of the Great War. He left behind his wife and three sons. Joseph Kaye was buried on 7th August, two days after his demise. Douglas was everything to him, cradle to grave: place of birth, education, employment and worship. It was where he raised his family; and what a proud legacy he left for the next generation![83]

At the service in the garden, I had placed an arrangement of sunflowers in front of the large memorial, alongside the Council's beautiful wreath of white roses. However, I like to lay something at the original memorial stone as well, and I had brought a single sunflower for that purpose. I haven't been able to pay my respects to either memorial for a few years because of personal circumstances, and for reasons beyond my control; but Douglas Borough council have been wonderful and have laid flowers on my behalf.

We walked along the promenade to our hotels, Jamie and I, engrossed in conversation. Decades apart in age, yet united by our interest in Summerland. We parted in front of the Palace, but the tragedy would continue to occupy our minds before it was finally time for sleep.

A few months later, Jamie sent me some postcards. These would form part of a display of fifty cards – each representing a life lost – for the final part of his project. Half the cards were originals from the early 1970s, and the other half were created using photographs taken during his time on the Island. Each of the latter had a quote from the inquiry on the back, while the rest were left blank for survivors and witnesses to write a few words. I received three. The first had an image of a church that is no longer there. It made me think of how the old must often give way to the new; like Derby Castle was demolished so Summerland could be built. The image on the second postcard was one I am familiar with, as it appears in a brochure advertising the new entertainment centre. I was given a perfectly preserved copy by a dear Manx friend. It is a treasured possession. One I could never part with.

The final card I drew out of the envelope had a photograph of the terminus of the tramway. It's an image that, for me, evokes many emotions as does the big white sign on the cliff, which was recently replaced. Between the terminus and the *Manx Electric Railway* sheds, the place that shaped my life once stood.

I wonder what the future holds for the derelict site and what impact it will have on the next generation; but only time will tell.

Chapter 14: Clowns Cry Too
"…I think I'll be six now for ever and ever!"[84]

The clowns I remember from childhood had big painted on smiles. They tripped over their huge clumsy shoes and often honked horns, which I hated because the noise made me jump. Braces held up baggy trousers, and some had a fake flower attached to their clothes. Anyone leaning over to sniff the delicate scent would be squirted with water, to the great delight of the audience!

I didn't know there were other clowns: those who couldn't smile. I wasn't aware that following the depression in America, several decades before my birth, a different kind of comic act had proved very popular with those who flocked to the circus.

***

The sad-faced clown dragged a big brush into the ring. He looked exhausted even before he began to sweep the earth floor in readiness for the next act. No matter how hard he tried, he couldn't sweep up a stubborn puddle of water; and this caused those watching to erupt into laughter. The object that defeated him was, in fact, a beam from one of the spotlights, which had been pointed towards the ground. The audience were able to laugh at the clown because they knew it was part of his performance. What they didn't know was that a time was coming when his sad demeanour would not be false, when his carefully applied make up would be streaked with dirt and tears. A time when people realised that clowns cry too.

***

In November 2017, I came across a blog about Summerland in

WordPress. Like Dr Ian Phillips, from the University of Birmingham, whose thorough research answered many questions I had about the fire, the author of the blog Ross Landy, first read about the tragedy in a book called *The Worst Disasters of the Twentieth Century*.[85]

I messaged Ross, when I finished reading. He replied immediately. The empathetic South African man and I have become firm friends, despite the many miles that separate us. Summerland is just one subject that Ross has written about. His accounts, which often feature disasters and their impact on those involved, are extremely informative and well-written. One struck a chord with me because, like the Manx fire, it happened in a place of entertainment.

***

There was great excitement in Hartford, Connecticut, during the first week of July 1944. The circus was coming to town!

Things usually ran according to plan because the circus folk were extremely well organised. They needed to be, as the show was the biggest in the land. Setting up the huge tent, and all that went with it, would have been an exhaustive process under normal circumstances; but America's participation in the war had led to a reduction in staff, which would have added to the pressure. Equipment was in short supply too.

A superstition among performers and management, may have meant that many of them were anticipating a disaster during the opening performance in Hartford. This was because the first of the two shows planned had to be axed due to the late arrival of the trains transporting the *Ringling Brothers and Barnum & Bailey Circus*. Missing a performance was thought to be a harbinger of ill luck. However, no calamity marred the first show, and everyone was able to breathe a sigh of relief.

The one thing there was no worry about, was rain falling on the thousands of spectators gathered beneath the canvas dome. In recognition of the unpredictability of the elements, the tent's roof had been treated, some months before, with a mix of paraffin wax and petrol/gasoline, which at that time was the usual method of waterproofing.

It was exactly one month after D-Day when the people of Hartford, and the surrounding area, made their way to the three-ring circus on Barbour Street for a matinee performance. The tent wasn't filled to capacity, just as Summerland hadn't been on the night of the fire. Around seven thousand spectators entered the Big Top, most of whom were women and children. Men who weren't involved in the war effort were probably still at work.

Other forms of entertainment were thin on the ground in the busy town of Hartford, and a visit to the circus was a much-anticipated event each summer. For a few hours, cares could be set aside, and minds distracted from what was going on in the rest of the world and loved ones who were far away.

Thursday 6th July was very hot. It was too hot, really, to be sitting elbow to elbow on the tiered benches, known as bleachers, breathing in the aroma of sawdust, animal sweat and sheer excitement. The big cats had just completed their act, and the Great Wallendas had taken the floor. They would shortly be in the air, causing hearts to leap; but the feeling of exhilaration that the famous trapeze artists elicited, would be short-lived. Terror was salivating in the wings, keen to turn pleasure to pain; desperate to introduce pandemonium to the innocent folk who had come to the circus as a treat.

Suddenly, the band broke into *The Stars and Stripes Forever*. It was a tune none of the circus staff or performers ever wanted to hear during a show because it meant that something had gone badly wrong! Vicious flames were surging up the wall on the tent's south-west side.

***

The man in the back yard wiped sweat from his brow. He was cutting wood – warm work at the best of times, but punishingly so on a scorching July afternoon. Sunshine glinted off his saw, and he could see the big top reflected in the blade. Suddenly, despite the intense heat, he felt chilled to the bone. The image had changed. It seemed as if the flaming globe above him had fallen to earth, filling the space previously occupied by the huge circus tent! He began to run.

Maureen Krekian was eleven years old in July 1944. Arrangements had been made that she would attend the circus with neighbours. However, when the time came she was disappointed to discover there was no one there when she called. The young girl knew that permission to go alone would never be granted, even though the showgrounds were on the same street. She had never been to the circus before and was determined not to miss out. Standing in front of the unanswered door, she made a decision.

The performance was less than thirty minutes old when Maureen heard yelling from her seat, midway up the bleachers. She saw a fireball close to the roof. It was increasing in size at a most incredible rate!

A small flame, believed to have been spotted by the band leader, which led to the playing of the circus distress signal, had rapidly developed into a blaze beyond the control of staff. Attempts were made to extinguish the fire with jugs of water and to rip away the burning canvas to halt its progress, but to no avail. The power failed, and no one heard the ringmaster's appeal for calm.

Many of those who fell in the stampede to escape the flames were trampled on. The blazing roof bled its protective coating, causing burns. The tent had a total of nine exits, including the main one, but some were blocked by the animal "chutes". Wagons were parked outside, waiting to take the big cats back to their enclosures and welcome refreshments. There was no way past. Maureen saw a man grabbing youngsters and hurling them over the top of the cages, out of reach of the furious, pawing beasts.

In Summerland, Noel Quigley, an Irishman, almost six and a half feet tall, grabbed dozens of children who were being trampled on in the panic and threw them out of an open door. Despite his height and great strength, Noel was knocked to the ground at one point, such was the hysteria in the building

Maureen was pulled to safety by a youth when she leapt down onto the straw-covered earth. The lad slashed the tent wall with his penknife and trailed her out. Maureen was able to catch hold of another child and bring her to safety too.

The bleachers were burned through. Photographs taken after fire had completed its rampage in Summerland, show that some of the wooden treads on the flying staircase were burned away. My mother and I ran up those stairs while flames ate through wood and flesh. They are images that both haunt me and make me realise just how lucky we were.

In both tragedies, parents searched frantically for their children, having become separated from them in the chaos. Some people, who had escaped from the circus tent at Hartford, rushed back in after failing to see the faces of their loved ones among the trembling, distressed survivors in the showgrounds. Less than ten minutes after the fire started, the huge tent collapsed. Many were still trapped inside. A number of people had remained in their seats, believing that the flames would be swiftly extinguished.

I have only been to the circus twice in my life. On the first occasion, I attended with my parents and sister. Youths kept lifting the bottom of the tent wall behind us to get in without paying. Light streamed in each time, and it was distracting. There was a fear that they'd get up no good. We didn't enjoy the show, and I knew that night that we would never be back as a family.

After many pleas from my children, a second visit to the circus occurred more than two decades later. My middle daughter volunteered to help the clown – something I would never have had the confidence, or the desire, to do when I was a child. I didn't want to dampen her enthusiasm by refusing to let her participate, but I realise now, that if disaster had struck, we could easily have become separated.

Maureen Krekian, speaking about the Hartford tragedy, more than six decades later, recalled her uncle's reaction and the look on his face when he discovered she was safe. It was anger mixed with joy and incredible relief; anger because things might have turned out very differently.

It would be many years before the circus paid a return visit to Hartford. Maureen didn't attend. This was the case with a lot of people who had been caught up in the tragedy.

I felt a huge lump form in my throat when Maureen spoke about the lad who pulled her to safety, and the fact that she wouldn't have made it out if it hadn't been for him. I feel the same way about the fireman who rescued us from Summerland. It seemed that hope was gone as Mum peered desperately from a broken pane of glass in the smoke-filled solarium. It was too high up for her to climb out. We were badly burned, suffering from smoke inhalation and in shock. With a weak voice, my mother managed to attract the attention of a fireman who was on the next level of the outdoor terrace. He hadn't been expecting to find any survivors where we were. I was raised by mum's trembling arms and pulled to safety by the strong arms of the fireman. If it hadn't been for those actions, I would not be a mother and a grandmother. I always hoped that, one day, I would be able to thank him in person, though a simple thank you can never be enough for the gift of a second chance at life. He and my mother gave me that.

Dorothy Carvey (Dot) returned to the circus for the first time sixty years after the tragedy. The lady and her three-year-old son were fortunate to escape with their lives. The pair were knocked to the ground and trodden on by others in the desperate race for survival. The actions of a circus attendant saved mother and son. The man dragged them from the burning tent, where exits were obscured by smoke. Mrs Carvey described him as "wonderful." She never discovered his identity.

When I read Dorothy Carvey's description of how she and her child made their perilous way down from their seats in the bleachers, I thought of Mum, who threw down her shoes and bag too, as they hindered her progress, and also because a young neighbour called her Dot when he was around the same age as Tighe Carvey. He may have been confused as her cousin's name was Dorothy, but for whatever reason, she was Dot to him for the rest of her life.

A photograph taken by a member of the audience, after the dreadful circus fire, shows a clown striding purposefully forward, despite the look of despair on his face. His surroundings could almost be described as post-apocalyptic. Emmet Kelly dressed in the costume of sad clown character Weary Willie – his own invention – is carrying a bucket of water. It was a drop in the ocean needed to quench the horror in Hartford that day. There is no doubt that he was one of the heroes of the tragedy. The brave man immediately rushed to the aid of spectators, holding up the canvas to help them escape. He did all in his power to bring people to safety, and to soothe distraught youngsters whose parents were missing.

The full impact of what had happened engulfed Emmett when it was time to leave. Warped poles and wires, the bare bones of the Big Top – like the skeletal remains of Summerland's solarium – were a stark testimony to the afternoon's terror. Scorched shoes lay amid the ruins, where laughter had so quickly turned to screams. The remainder of a beloved toy caught his eye: a clown doll; the fate of its little owner unknown. He broke down.

Emmet Kelly continued in his role for a further ten years. He likened the effect the tragedy had on him to "a movie forever playing in his mind"; one he was powerless to stop. He didn't speak often about his experience; it was too painful. Only with his family, was he able to break his silence.

An estimated one hundred and sixty-seven people perished in the circus fire – the cause of which has never been established – and around seven hundred sustained injuries, consisting of burns and broken bones. Miraculously, survivors were found beneath piles of bodies close to some exits. A few of those who died remained unidentified. A little girl captured hearts across America when her photograph was circulated in attempt to establish her identity. Two detectives worked tirelessly on the case for years. The dedicated gentlemen tended her grave with fresh flowers several times a year, including Christmas and Independence Day, until they too passed away. Each victim of the fire was given a number at the temporary morgue set up in the wake of the disaster, and because of this the unknown child was called Little Miss 1565.[86]

One father identified his young daughter by her red shoes – ruby slippers – like Dorothy in the movie, Wizard of Oz. The shoes are much treasured by Carolyn's family.[87]

On July 6th, 1944, a little girl woke up full of excitement because it was her birthday. She was six years old and would be celebrating at her home, which was far away from America but close to where American service men were stationed. She never forgot the kindness of those young men, known as GIs, who always had chewing gum and candy for the neighbouring youngsters. Local people arranged social evenings and dances for them, so they wouldn't be lonely so far from their homes and families.

When darkness fell over the cottage on the Bog Road, which backed onto Long Kesh airbase, Muriel was drifting off to sleep. She was tired after a day of fun with her cousin and oblivious of the terrible fire that had occurred in Hartford, where children her age had died. Twenty-nine years later – a time so far away that she could not begin to imagine it, she would be a married lady with children of her own, one of whom would be in her sixth year; a little girl who always saw a rainbow in the sky, whatever the weather. The family of four would set off on a big adventure across the Irish Sea, brimful of happiness because a dream was coming true…

[A memorial, consisting of bronze plaques, each bearing information about the tragic fire in Hartford, was dedicated on 6th July 2005. A central plaque is situated where the middle ring of the circus would have been. It is inscribed with the name of each person who died on that dreadful day.][88]

Chapter 15: Dolphins and Finchley

Of thy children, some have wandered,
Far away across the main,
But their love of Ellan Vannin
Softly calls them back again.

(From *Isle of Mona* by John W. Gelling)

The kite made several feeble attempts to lift off the ground before collapsing, defeated. Suddenly, a gust of wind snatched it up, and it was off!

Sam watched his parents with pleasure. It was as if the kite had taken away all their cares when it soared into the blue sky above their beautiful island home.

It was the kind of moment you want to last forever: surrounded by those most dear to you, everyone safe and happy; but things can't stay the same. Two more little girls would join the Webb family – sisters for baby Rachel, who was fast asleep in her carrycot on that perfect evening at the Point of Ayre.

***

Samuel was a popular name in the Webb family as it is in mine. When a new baby boy was born in 1937, he was given the name of his forebears. His father and grandfather were also Samuel, and it was the first name of his great-great-grandfather, who had once been mayor of Douglas.

The late Samuel Webb JP was born in Cheshire. He moved to the Isle of Man in the 1850s, where his experience in selling jewellery and ornamental goods enabled him to set up shop in Strand Street.

Some years later, the businessman became involved in the entertainment industry. Webb's Lounge was a huge attraction for the residents of Victorian Douglas and further afield. It boasted an impressive glazed arcade and not only had an organ, but an orchestra as well to provide music for the tea dances, which were all the rage!

"It was the place to be seen," said Sam.

A photograph that appeared in a supplement to the *Isle of Man Weekly Times*, 12th June 1903, shows Mr Webb, resplendent in the full regalia of First Citizen of the Borough. He served several terms as mayor, between 1898 and 1902. The latter just a year before his death. The photograph was printed to commemorate his passing, which occurred on Friday 5th June; burial took place four days later.

Sam and his dad visited Old Braddan churchyard to look for their ancestor's final resting place, but their search was futile. It wasn't until after his father's death, that Sam found the grave in new Braddan cemetery and was able to pay his respects to his great-great-grandfather, and to all the other relatives that he discovered were interred there.

The late mayor was not the only member of the Webb family who provided entertainment for the public. Sam's great-great-aunt left home at the age of sixteen in search of excitement. She found it when she joined a circus show based in Manchester. The act she was part of was dangerous to say the least! Brave Katy stood still while knives were thrown at her. Sam's father told him that she was also spun on a wheel as the knives were thrown. Katy Hyslop proved that fortune does indeed favour the brave! She lived to the grand age of one hundred and four!

Sam grew up in East Finchley through the difficult war years and their aftermath. He was a lively infant and often caused his mother to come rushing out of the family shop to see what he was up to! At the end of the war, Sam's grandfather came to visit and brought him a Manx cat. "She was a lovely cat," he told me. A plethora of kittens were born. Each litter was different. Some were Manx cats, like their mum, while others had stumpy tails. Ancestors of Sam's pet still pop up in the area every now and then!

On a June evening, in 1949, Sam set off on a great adventure with his dad. They boarded the all-night train to Lime Street Station, but neither of them slept. When they stepped, blinking, onto the platform, the day was fresh and new. Night had been swept away while the train chuffed towards its destination. An infant sun illuminated St George's Hall – a splendid example of neoclassical architecture – which greeted those leaving the station to begin their adventures, including a little boy for whom architecture would become a career years later.

Sam was beside himself with excitement as the Mona's Isle ploughed steadily towards his father's homeland. The boiled egg sandwiches, made by his mum for the journey, were long gone and his lemonade too; consumed in the mistaken belief that the ferry that crossed the River Mersey was taking him to the Isle of Man! Mr Webb made up the shortfall by buying his son a Toblerone!

Sam's first glimpse of the Island was etched in his memory. It was "magical," he said, describing his experience as an eleven-year-old lad: the clarity of the water, one of the crew flying the Manx flag, the reaction of the other passengers, and in the distance, the summit of Snaefell.

"I'd never seen anything like that before," he told me. "We were accompanied by dolphins. You didn't get dolphins in East Finchley!"

The youngster watched as motorbikes roared off the Isle of Man boat. They were there for the TT races as were he and his dad.

Sam and his father stayed at the home of a bus inspector, who had been directing traffic when Mr Webb approached him to enquire about accommodation. The father and son were treated as members of the family in the house on Westmoreland Road, where the garden was full of flowers – the inspector had green fingers. Sam recalls spectacular red-hot pokers and the inspector's wife giving him a Mars Bar as a treat. They arrived back one evening to the news that a telegram was waiting at the post office. Sam had passed his Eleven Plus! His academic prowess was rewarded with a ten-shilling note from his grandfather

Another memorable moment was lunch at the *Bungalow* on the TT course. Sam chose poached egg on toast, "an absolute luxury," he said!

While enjoying another meal, this time in a Douglas restaurant, Sam overheard two ladies talking about the races. They were discussing lap times and riders. One young rider stood out to them. His name was Geoff Duke!

Sam made the acquaintance of other Manx relatives during that unforgettable holiday, including a cousin of his father's. He, too, was called Sam. Photographs were taken outside the Gaiety Theatre, treasured mementoes of a wonderful time.

Sam took his little daughters to the Isle of Man to experience many of the things that made his childhood holiday so enjoyable. Silverdale Glen was their first stop, and the girls loved the Victorian water-powered roundabout. They said hello to the little people when crossing the Fairy Bridge, rode on the steam train and travelled on the Manx Electric Railway to see Lady Isabella – the Great Laxey Wheel. A horse tram carried the excited children along Douglas Promenade, while the sun shone down on them. They even liked kippers, said Sam.

My father longed to do the same, but our holiday was cut cruelly short. I have done nearly all the things that he enjoyed so much during trips to the Island in his youth. Things that he wanted his little girls to experience in the summer of 1973. One thing remains undone, though, and I think it might have to stay that way. Manx kippers were on the menu most days for Dad, who really loved fish. Unfortunately, neither of his girls have taken after him!

In 1969, when Mr and Mrs Webb senior made the Isle of Man their permanent home, the construction of Summerland was underway. On July 14th that year, the sub-contract tender for the Oroglas cladding was accepted. W. J. Cox, Hertfordshire, would mould the acrylic panels, supplied by Lennig Chemicals Ltd., Jarrow (a subsidiary of Rohm and Haas, Philadelphia), to the required specification.[89]

When Sam travelled to the Island, to watch the TT races and spend time with his parents, in June 1971, he didn't visit Summerland. Two years later, he was one of the many people trying desperately to contact loved ones in the wake of the disaster. Jammed telephone lines meant it was three or four days before he got through. Mr and Mrs Webb were safe at home in Ramsey on that terrible night. Despite this, they were reluctant to talk about the fire, and when Sam's father passed away, his mother firmly changed the subject if it came up! Neither of them had ever been inside the tragic building.

Sam Webb contacted me in 2017, following the horrific blaze at Grenfell Tower. He explained that he had delivered a paper to RIBA – the Royal Institute of British Architects – on the subject of Summerland just after the fire commission's report was published in 1974. He drew my attention to one of the points made in the report: the lack of understanding about fire among architects.

In 1975, Sam began to give lectures on construction at the School of Architecture in Canterbury. When he asked the post graduate students, who had attended schools of architecture around the world, if any of their past lectures had covered fire, it was a very "rare" occasion if anyone raised their hand. A quarter of the lectures Sam gave each year were on fires in buildings, and how they had led to important changes in legislation. He mentioned some of the changes wrought because of lives lost: "unit widths of escape," fire-proof safety curtains and fire escapes that have doors that open outwards. One of the fatal fires Sam lectured on, occurred at the Iroquois Theatre in Chicago, Illinois.

The Renaissance-style Iroquois Theatre, on West Randolph Street, had been open for less than six weeks when tragedy struck. Building work had been running behind but was hurried along to ensure the theatre opened by the start of the holiday season.

Christmas was quickly becoming a distant memory as the jagged cold of January loomed. Only one full day of 1903 remained, when people flocked to the magnificent building to watch a matinee performance of *Mr Blue Beard*. Women and children made up a substantial part of the audience. The outing should have been a lovely treat. School would soon resume, and it would be a while before there was something to look forward to again.

Every ticket, including those for standing room, had been sold (around sixteen hundred seated and just over one hundred standing tickets). Afterwards, it was estimated there were two thousand or more in the audience that day. Actor Eddie Foy hadn't been able to get tickets for his family, but he decided to bring his little boy anyway. A place was found for him near the stage.

The theatre was sixty feet tall from floor to ceiling and elaborately decorated. It was the last word in elegance. Patrons were accommodated on three levels: the main floor, at entrance level – referred to as the Orchestra or Parquet – and two balconies.

Just fifteen minutes into the second half of the performance, fire ripped through the Iroquois Theatre, which had been advertised as "absolutely fireproof." A spark from one of the lights used to create an effect on stage caused some muslin to ignite. Dry fire extinguishers proved useless. Painted props found favour with probing tongues of flame. Burning scenery dropped on those below. Smoke and fumes were unable to escape through roof flues, which had been fastened with nails. Actors and crew ran for a door at the rear of the stage. Chilly air was admitted as they made their exit. A fireball took advantage of the gap beneath the fire curtain, which had caught on a wire when it was being lowered. Over the heads of those in the orchestra section it went. They sprang from their seats and fled. Many people ran to the foyer, known as the "Grand Stair

Hall" and made for the front door – a natural response – as it was the way they had entered the building.

There was no salvation for anything in the path of the seething cloud of destruction. Some poor souls in the balconies were "trapped" in their seats. Those who made it to the stairs encountered locked gates at the bottom. The folding metal barriers stopped people creeping to the lower level and the more expensive seats. There were thirty emergency exits, a number of which had to be forced open from the inside or by people outside. Most didn't understand how the locks worked. Some doors were concealed by curtains. On the North side of the building were emergency exits that opened onto fire escapes. The ledges were narrow. The doors of the exits below blocked the way of those coming down. Casualties mounted up on the icy ground. Bodies broke the fall of others.

Workmen in a room in a Northwestern University building – there had been a fire there, too – on the opposite side of the alley, pushed out a ladder to "bridge" the gap between the two buildings. Planks gave it strength. Some were saved in this way, but others fell to their deaths.

When the fire brigade arrived, they concentrated on rescuing the people on the escapes, though their mission was fraught with difficulty. Couch Place was less than twenty feet wide and full of smoke, which concealed the life net from the person who would be jumping and conversely, firemen from "jumper."

Eddie Foy had sent his son to safety with a stagehand, when it was clear that the fire was out of control. He hadn't been able to leave himself after looking towards the audience, which seemed full of innocent little faces – even though burning debris rained down on him. He appealed for calm and urged the orchestra to play on, but when that ball of fire shot across the room, he knew that nothing more could be done.

Flames illuminated the darkened theatre when the fuse box succumbed to the blaze.

Many were knocked down and trampled on in the panic. Bodies piled up on the Parquet floor as people jumped from the balconies to escape the raging flames. A fire marshal calling out, received no answering cry. Hope that there were survivors buried in the deep piles of bodies was crushed.

Some six hundred people died in the blazing theatre and many more were injured. All that remained of the stage was a "steel skeleton." Most of the cast and crew were saved; possibly because fire escaped under the curtain meant to contain it.

A stagehand was sent to get help as there was no telephone or fire alarm in the building. Although an engine was dispatched immediately, the lack of both may have cost precious minutes.

The recovery operation began. Tiny bodies were carried from the ruins as firemen, police officers and members of the public wept. A nearby diner was commandeered as a hospital and make-shift morgue. Distraught friends and relatives arrived seeking loved ones. Relief at not finding a familiar face among the dead was often temporary, as more bodies were recovered and taken to other locations around the city.

All theatres in Chicago and further afield were closed until safety checks could be made.

A local paper reported issues which may have contributed to the disaster, including the absence of a satisfactory fire alarm, the lack of sprinklers and signs indicating exits.

Important and lasting safety measures came about because of the tragedy. A red light over exits would guide people to safety if power failed elsewhere. Nowadays, most signs are green. The *running man* indicates the route we should take. How many people know the human cost of that seemingly simple device? I didn't, and I feel deeply ashamed.

A gentleman who had planned to attend the ill-fated performance was horrified by the dreadful loss of life. Work commitments meant that Carl Prinzler, a hardware salesman, had to change his plans. Mr

Prinzler, from Philadelphia, was disturbed that the audience, when fleeing for their lives at the Iroquois Theatre, encountered exits they couldn't open. He came up with a solution which he developed with architectural engineer, Henry H. Dupont. Their product was ready to be marketed in 1908. This was done by Vonnegut Hardware Company. "The Panic Bar," would prevent doors from being opened on the outside, while the pressure of pushing against the mechanism in an emergency, ensured that it opened easily from inside. Von Duprin was the name it would be sold under – a nod to each of the gentleman who brought it into being.

I remember looking at the panic bars on fire doors at school and wondering how they worked and hoping, at the same time, that I never had the occasion to find out. I knew where all the fire exits were in school. I carefully note the location of emergency exits everywhere I go. As Eddie Foy said after his terrible ordeal, "It takes a disaster to make one cautious."

The theatre reopened with a new name, around a year later. It was demolished in 1924 and another theatre was built in its place.

Seven years after the tragic fire, the Iroquois Memorial Hospital was dedicated to those who perished. It was built with the aid of money raised by the Iroquois Memorial Association. A speech was made by the commissioner of health at the same time of day that the fire occurred. During his tribute to the victims, he said, "It is well that they should not have died in vain, but that some good should come out of their sacrifice and suffering."

A photograph taken in January 1904, shows a group of gentlemen standing in the Iroquois Theatre, surveying the destruction caused by the fire. I find it terribly poignant, as it reminds me of a similar photo, taken after the Summerland disaster, over seventy years later. I wonder how many more photographs like this there will be: images of perplexed people, trying to figure out where it all went wrong![90]

People must be made aware, the lessons from the past *must* be learned. Too many lives have been sacrificed at the altar of ignorance.

***

[When Sam told me about dolphins swimming alongside the boat as they sailed towards Douglas, I thought of a passage I read in a book, a long time ago. The author said dolphins must keep moving when they're ill, or they won't survive. Other dolphins come to their aid, nudging them along until they recover. At a very low point, I remembered that story and thought of the wonderful friends I've made because of the tragedy at Summerland. They knew a better time would come and kept me going when I felt like giving up. "A bit of dolphin work," that's what it was.][91]

Chapter 16: Beyond the Rainbow

A beautiful princess looked from the top window of a tower at the terrifying dragon below. It opened its huge mouth to reveal a fiery furnace. Soon, flames were creeping up the tower's outer wall towards her as she watched in despair. Just then, the princess heard a noise in the distance.

The faint sound of galloping hooves became louder, and those gathered outside, watching helplessly, saw a handsome knight on a gleaming horse. The bystanders felt relief surge through them. The dragon would be slain, then the brave knight, having vanquished the foe, could rescue the petrified princess.

To their great surprise, the knight, once dismounted, did not immediately draw his powerful sword. After glancing at the flames speeding towards the girl, he dashed past the dragon and into the tower, where he encountered thick smoke and incredible heat. He battled on.

Finally, with his precious bundle in his arms, he began to descend the stairs. Smoke stung his eyes and threatened to choke them both. At last, there was a chink of light. Safely outside, well away from the tower, the pair watched as flames continued to devour everything in sight. Before long, they had reached the window where the princess had been standing just a short while before. The dragon continued to vent its fury until it expired.

The knight knew that the situation would have worsened with every second he spent fighting the beast. There would be other dragons in the future, and there was nothing he could do about that. He realised, however, that the best way to defeat them was to be prepared, to have measures in place that would stop a dragon in its tracks before lives were put in danger. It would be a huge undertaking, and he'd need a lot of help, but he would do it no matter what. Life is so precious.

Books are my escape from reality. During frequent childhood illnesses, while other children played outside, I lay in bed with the curtains drawn. The pile of books on my bedside table cheered me up in a way nothing else could. I loved fairy tales, though I found some of the illustrations frightening. I used to make up my own stories, which often featured beautiful princesses, dastardly dragons and brave knights. The fireman who pulled my mother and I from Summerland was my knight. In the tales I invented, he climbed the stairs to our rescue before the dragon breathed destruction upon us, stripping flesh from bone. My imagination was the only place there could be a happy ending!

Summerland was enjoying its second season in 1972. Many of those who came to enjoy the vast variety of activities in the popular venue, walked along the promenade and crossed over the King Edward Road via the concrete bridge safe from traffic and trams. The design of the bridge appeals to me, but unfortunately I didn't have an opportunity to visit it before it was demolished.

In North Kensington, in 1972, a high-rise building was under construction. The Brutalist-style tower, which would have twenty-four floors, was designed five years before – the year Summerland's architects visited an exhibition in Montreal, where they were particularly impressed by the American Pavilion – a geodesic dome – the work of Buckminster Fuller and Shoji Sadao. Five months later, an initial application was made for bye-law approval concerning the design of the Isle of Man's new entertainment complex. There were three applications in total. Plans accompanying the first, showed that concrete would be used in the construction of the east wall and the east end of the south-facing wall.[92]

When the second bye-law submission was made in July, the following year, concrete had been replaced with Galbestos, which would be attached to a metal frame.[93] A void was created when the amusement arcade on the other side was fitted with decalin (to give it a more soundproof finish than plasterboard).[94] When gases from the kiosk fire ignited in the void, fire was able to develop unseen until it burst into the arcade.

The commission appointed to investigate the Summerland disaster made thirty-four recommendations. Number fifteen relates to voids. It stated that those "with combustible interior surfaces should not be unnecessarily incorporated into a building intended for public assembly." If voids are "functionally essential," sprinklers and "reliable fire stopping" should be in place.[95]

It was recommended that sprinklers should be installed in all large buildings. Alan Christian explained that the purpose of a sprinkler system is to detect fire and keep it "in check." Regarding the blaze in Summerland, retired firefighter, Godfrey Cain believes that the presence of sprinklers may have resulted in a "much smaller fire."

The Summerland blaze led to legislative changes both in the Isle of Man and the United Kingdom.

Three years after the tragedy, the *Summerland Amendments* were passed in the House of Commons. The new law was intended to protect the lives of those who lived or worked in large buildings. It decreed that the external walls of such structures must be fire resistant.

The Fires That Foretold Grenfell, which was shown on BBC Two in October 2018, features five fires that, between them, address the issues of lack of fire resistance in external walls, combustible cladding, fire stopping, the absence of sprinklers and delayed evacuation.

The first fire discussed in the programme is Summerland.

When Godfrey Cain saw images of the blazing London Tower, he thought, "…not again!"

The bell that signalled the end of Godfrey's plans for an evening out with his wife, on 2nd August 1973, sounded shortly after 8:00 pm. He rushed to the fire station, where the young Control operator updated him with the words: "It's Summerland!"

When the engine turned off Victoria Street, the firemen realised that catastrophe had claimed the complex. Godfrey stared at the vast cloud of black smoke looming above Summerland, and the flames consuming the roof from end to end. "It's the big one," he said.

The fire vented its fury when the men entered the building. Godfrey, who went in via the main entrance likened the sound to a steam train rushing through a station.

"People don't realise that fire is a living thing, it breathes, and it roars, you feel it," he explained.

Despite the lava-like acrylic falling from the roof, the men crossed the Solarium floor spraying jets of water as they went.

Great gulps of oxygen, admitted when the Oroglas panels burned away, fed the flames.

"We didn't put this fire out," declared Godfrey. "The fire burnt itself out."

All the other fires discussed in the programme occurred in high-rise buildings.

The fire at Knowsley Heights in 1991, was the first tower block cladding fire in Great Britain. Like Summerland, the fire started externally. Youths ignited some old furniture that had been dumped at the foot of the building. Flames spread up the side of the eleven-storey structure in Huyton, Liverpool, via the cladding, which had been installed in order to resolve the issue of damp. A gap between cladding and wall acted as a chimney. Fortunately, there were no fatalities. The blaze should have taught a valuable lesson.

In 1999, a blaze at Garnock Court, Irvine, North Ayrshire, claimed the life of a wheelchair-bound resident who had dropped his cigarette. The fourteen-storey structure was one of five high-rises in the area that had cladding installed for cosmetic purposes. Although there had been fires in the buildings prior to the renovations, they had been "contained," and there were no complications.

Flames spread to the cladding panel through the window of the flat on the fifth floor, which ignited the panel above and so on. The progression of flames up the side of the building was rapid.

Six years later, three lives were claimed by a fire in Harrow Court, Stevenage. A couple had gone to sleep leaving tea lights burning on top of a television set in their bedroom. They melted into it, causing a rapidly developing fire. Firefighters were able to save the life of the male resident, but the two young men, just at the beginning of their career in the service, lost their own lives trying to save his partner.

Advice had been to "stay put." Another resident on the fourteenth floor of the seventeen-storey block, initially heeded this advice, but concerned that the situation was worsening, and fearful for her children's safety, she decided to leave with her young family. They made it out.

There were no sprinklers installed at Harrow Court.

Tragedy came to Lakanal House on a warm Saturday afternoon in July 2009. A fault in a television started a fire in the tower block in Camberwell. Advice to residents who called the fire service was to stay put. Catherine Hickman, a dressmaker, resided on the floor above the flat where the fire started. She spent forty minutes on the telephone to an emergency operator, asking for guidance and expressing concern for her neighbours. Catherine died in her home – flat seventy-nine.

A family on the same floor as Catherine survived after going against advice when they saw smoke coming through a vent in a bathroom, where they were sheltering. Other residents, who had taken refuge with them, remained in the flat. They weren't so lucky.

Six lives were lost in the Lakanal House fire.

It may be safer in some instances to *stay put* rather than venture into the unknown, but this depends on compartmentalisation being successful.

Godfrey Cain's opinion since the fire in Summerland is "If you have a fire you get people out."[96]

On 14th June 2017, a fridge that had an electrical fault started a fire in the kitchen of a fourth floor flat in Grenfell Tower. What happened next sent shock waves across the world.

Marco Gottardi and Gloria Trevisan moved to London from Italy in the spring of 2017. The young architects, who met at university, were bowled over by what the city had to offer, and it wasn't long before they found jobs and made friends. Their home on the twenty-third floor of Grenfell Tower was cosy and inviting, and the views were stunning. Marco's parents visited once they had settled in and saw, to their delight, how enchanted the couple were with their new life.

Daniela and Giannino were looking forward to their son's June birthday and had planned many festivities to mark the occasion. While making the arrangements and issuing invitations, they had no idea that the passing time was not bringing them closer to a reunion with Marco and his lovely girlfriend, but creeping towards tragedy, death and destruction.

There can be nothing worse than a telephone ringing in the early hours. Unless happy news is expected, by way of a new addition to a family, the call usually brings news that is devastating. Such was the call that Daniela received from Gloria's distressed mother in the small hours of June 14th, 2017. Grenfell tower was on fire!

Daniela and Giannino weren't asleep when the phone rang. They had been putting the final touches to preparations for their holiday, as it was almost time for them to leave for the airport. Now, the luggage packed in anticipation of a pleasant break in Sicily, was no longer needed. Their whole focus was on the telephone and the news it would bring from their beloved son, their only child, their whole world.

As the minutes ticked by, any hope that he would be ok, that he and Gloria would be led to safety, away from the smoke and flames, as Marco had initially believed, faded.

Images of the blazing tower, that appeared on the television, filled them with horror.

After Marco's frantic phone call, in which he explained to his parents that they had finally been told to evacuate the building – but had been unable to leave due to the heat and thick smoke – Giannino received a voicemail. It was from his son. Marco wanted to tell his parents how much he loved them. The months rolled back, Daniela, in her anguish, remembered the last time she had held her precious boy. That hug, before boarding the plane home in April, was like no other they had ever shared.

Giannino called his son's number relentlessly, but there was no response.

The words spoken by Gloria Trevisan to her mother Emanuela, in the last minutes of her life, haunt me. The beautiful young woman had so much to live for. Gloria and Marco had been fulfilling their dream. Nothing was impossible for them. Gloria thanked her mother for everything she had done for her. She expressed sorrow that she could never put her arms around Emanuela again; she railed against the unfairness of what was happening. Gloria told her mother that she didn't "want to die."

When an announcement was made in Summerland, telling people not to panic, my father, who always respected authority, hesitated briefly before instinct took over. If he hadn't made the decision to lead us out when he did, our story may have been very different.

Marco Gottardi also respected authority. He would never have disobeyed advice given by the fire service. His parents would later discover that some of those who lived on the same floor survived, because they had decided to leave, contrary to what they'd been told.

Gloria and Marco died with their arms around one another. Marco was twenty-seven years old and Gloria, twenty-six.

I was incredibly moved when I discovered that Marco's mother has written a children's book in tribute to the young couple. The brave knight, Marco, rescues the princess (Gloria), who is threatened by a dragon's fiery breath. Leaving the tower, which was her home, far behind, she lives happily with her handsome knight in a peaceful place filled with pretty flowers and fluttering butterflies. It had to turn out that way for Daniela to be able to cope with her terrible loss. Sometimes, the truth is just too much to bear.

One of the final images Gloria Trevisan captured of the view from her new home, showed a beautiful rainbow in the grey London sky. The rainbow: a symbol of hope, a reminder that there are better times ahead. If we don't believe that, how can we carry on?[97]

A little boy is celebrating his birthday. Brightly coloured banners, pinned to the wall, tell us that he is five years old. Isaac stands proudly before a table laden with party food in his lovely home. Candles flicker on his cake which is chocolate flavoured with stars on it!

Isaac was a popular child, much thought of by teachers and schoolfriends. He excelled at everything he did – a real star, with "so much potential." His father was excited to see what the future held for his precious first-born son, but little Isaac had no future. His fifth birthday celebration would be his last. Isaac perished in the smoke-filled Grenfell Tower after his family were, at last, told to evacuate.

The night had begun like any other for Paulos Tekle and his family. His little boys had gone to bed without fuss, as they always did, and were soon fast asleep. It wasn't long before the whole family were sleeping soundly. However, the calm of flat 153, on the eighteenth floor of the tower, was shattered by a commotion in the communal hallway. Roused from peaceful slumber, Paulos went to see what wrong. He discovered from the distressed residents he encountered, that flames were shooting up the side of the building. Paulos immediately called the emergency services. He said he was "told to wait," that the Fire Brigade knew about the situation and would come for them.

Neighbours telephoned constantly, begging the family to make their escape. Paulos called the Fire Brigade again and again The passing of time was almost audible, bringing them closer to disaster minute by minute. At 2:00 am, it seemed that salvation had come, when they heard a knock on the door. However, when Paulos opened it, rather than be told to gather his precious family and leave, he was advised to put a blanket against the door and continue to wait.

At one point, Mr Tekle and his partner contemplated jumping from the balcony, hoping that they might be able to cushion the children with their own bodies.

Another three quarters of an hour went by before the call they were desperate for, came. It was time to go.

Their descent was extremely difficult due to dense smoke, but finally the little group made it out. Then, dreadful realisation dawned. Isaac was gone.

I thought of my poor dad, when I read that Isaac's frantic parents were held back as they tried to go back into the blazing tower to search for him. The same thing happened to him at Summerland.

In the days that followed, Isaac's parents visited hospitals in the desperate hope they would find their son amidst the injured. It wasn't until a few years ago, that I discovered my father was sent to the hospital morgue to look for Mum and I.

When he made enquiries after arriving at Noble's, Dad was directed to a room that was in darkness by a hard-pushed member of staff. He managed to locate a light switch, and the shock, when he realised that he was not in a ward with the injured, stayed with him the rest of his life. I cannot begin to imagine how he must have felt when his tear-filled eyes roamed the room, dreading that he might see a small form among the rest. And if his worse fears had been realised, what then? It is beyond my comprehension.

Isaac's mother and father discovered their son's fate on the news. I can't bear to think of him, just five years old, alone in the smoke, terrified, like I was in Summerland. Mr Tekle had carried his younger child as they made their way down the stairs. He believed that another man was holding Isaac's hand. The little boy's body was recovered from the thirteenth floor.

When Paulos Tekle found out that the tower block was on fire, he had telephoned friends in the building, who were still asleep. They left immediately and got out safely.

"I listened to the authorities," said Paulos, "and that makes me angry."[98]

Whatever peace I found by writing *Made in Summerland* was shattered the moment I saw the blazing London tower block on the television screen. I will never get those images out of my mind or forget all the people who perished.

I had hoped there would never be another Summerland; there must *never* be another Grenfell.

Chapter 17: A Time to Talk

Nine-year-old Julie, from Belfast, settled into her seat and waited for the show to begin. The cheerful striped deckchairs were occupied with other holidaymakers, who were eagerly waiting too. They might have been on the promenade; such was the outdoor feeling of the big building attached to the cliff face. It was the final night of the Colvin family's holiday on the Isle of Man, and they had chosen to spend it in Summerland.

Julie remembers her mum chatting to her about the dancers just before a sheet of flame shot across the room. Julie and her parents made their escape among a throng of people. They were fortunate to get out without difficulty. Some encountered exits that were locked.

Most of those fleeing the rapidly spreading fire, ran to the door they had entered by. This meant the area around the turnstiles quickly became congested, and some people were knocked over and trampled on.

There was no sign of Julie's younger brother, who had been watching cartoons. Mr Colvin turned to go back into Summerland to search for his son, and at that moment the boy was brought out by a couple.

"We were very lucky," said Julie, of her family's escape from the fire.

The Colvins arrived in Belfast the following day, where news crews were waiting at the docks. They wanted to speak to holidaymakers who had witnessed or been caught up in the tragedy. Mr Colvin was one of those interviewed.

Once safely home, the fire was "never discussed," Julie told me. In a message, in 2016, she said that in all the years since the disaster, her conversation with me was "the most" she had ever talked about it. In January, the same year, Julie came across an article on Facebook, which she found upsetting.

The subject was a potential new indoor venue in London. I was taken aback when I looked at the photograph that accompanied the article. It reminded me so much of the cliff face at Summerland, with the waterfall running down it. Money was being raised for the project through *Crowdfunding*.

The "tropical wonderland," at an undisclosed location, would have rock walls, a lagoon, hot tubs and beach huts too. When I read that, I couldn't help thinking of some of the original ideas for Summerland, based on a Cornish village theme with "an artificial Mediterranean climate." The seashore did not materialise, but deckchairs, palm trees and umbrella covered tables provided a seaside vibe. Plans for a lagoon also fell by the wayside, but the Aquadrome, next door, was handy for a dip. I noted several other similarities. The London venue would be convenient to public transport, just as the Manx complex had been close to the horse tramway and the electric railway. Visitors could "roam freely" in the "jungle paradise" and peruse the many "attractions" at their leisure. Summerland echoed in those words. A DJ would provide music, and those inclined could take in a show. Although the roof would not be transparent, the stars could still twinkle down thanks to modern technology.

The "brainchild" of Deborah Armstrong, described as "Characterful, authentic and original" – different from "any other event in the world – would be constructed like a film set. Controlled lighting and *weather* making it possible to escape from the miserable British winter without having to fly off in search of the sun.

I recently watched a video, during which this new "immersive" experience was described by its designer. I focused on the images on the screen. One gave me a jolt, as it called to mind the Rustic Walkway in Summerland, Isle of Man. I had imagined that climbing the wooden stairs to the Garden Bar would be like climbing up to a treehouse in the jungle! The images faded when I heard words that I found disturbing. I thought of the youngsters separated from their parents on the night of the fire because of the layout of the building. Those children had been happy and enjoying their adventure until the horror began. Then, I recalled the thirty-second recommendation made by the fire commission[99] and told myself, firmly, that things are different now. They are, aren't they!

What name would be given to this exciting new concept in England's capital city? It be would be called *Summerland*...[100]

Heidi, a dancer in Summerland, Douglas, recalls mummies and daddies searching frantically for children as fire ravaged the building. On entering the complex, excited youngsters parted from parents. Small figures disappeared downstairs in pursuit of pleasure. There was no fear for their safety. Everyone was under one roof.

Heidi's troupe were about to open the show on the Solarium's main floor, when an increase in activity around the amusement arcade attracted their attention. She remembers someone saying there was nothing to be concerned about, that people shouldn't panic. Everything was under control! Seconds later, the "nightmare began."

Although she has tried to block out those awful memories, Heidi cannot forget the screams or the desperation of those trapped on the balconies. She saw people preparing to jump, risking serious injury, or worse; but they had no choice.

Stunned by the terrifying turn of events, Heidi attempted to go to the dressing rooms to collect her things. People were running in "all directions," many with melted Oroglas clinging to their clothes and skin. Then she found herself shoved through a glass door – this, she believes, may have saved her life.

Still in deep shock, Heidi attempted to contact her family, but jammed phone lines prevented her from bringing them the reassurance they yearned for.

There might have been a tragic outcome for Heidi's loved ones, if it hadn't been for a change of plan. The dancers usually opened the cabaret show on the first terrace, escape from which was exceedingly difficult. During the emotional roll call at the Palace Hotel, Heidi discovered the fate of her colleagues. An event she found as distressing as the fire itself. A drummer, who had been playing in the Showbar, where Heidi might have been, didn't survive.

For Heidi, the smell of smoke or a clap of thunder cause horrible memories to come flooding back.

Roger McCune was fourteen years old when he visited the Isle of Man with his parents. The beautiful island made quite an impression, and a few years later he returned there to work during the holiday season.

After a spell in Howstrake Camp in Onchan and in a hotel on Loch Promenade, Roger was employed as a waiter in the Crescent. It was a very special time in his life, and he made many friends. A photograph shows all the staff, smart in their uniforms – a big happy family! Roger worked hard, and on his evenings off he enjoyed spending time at the Palace Lido and casino. The young man watched Summerland being built and visited the complex often when it opened.

On the morning of 3rd August 1973, Roger emerged from an uneasy sleep in his room at the Crescent to the sound of a helicopter hovering overhead. Although they'd closed before time, staff had pondered the events of the evening until the early hours. When they finally went to bed, they were unaware of the scale of the disaster that had befallen the entertainment centre. They had no idea that people had lost their lives.

At around 8:00 pm, the previous night, those who worked at the Crescent discovered there was a fire at Summerland. At that point, the "thin trails of smoke" that were visible did not indicate the severity of the situation. That soon changed.

Stunned people began to fill up the bar. They had been making their way along the promenade from the shocking scene at Summerland, chilled, despite the heat of the blaze. In the warmth and "normality" of the Toby Jug Bar, they told their dreadful tales. Mugs of hot tea warmed hands and eased shock. The music was switched off. It wasn't needed anymore.

Roger remembers the anguish of one lady, who had become separated from her family. Sadly, this was the case for many that night.

Hughie McAteer, who passed away some years ago, worked with Roger at the Crescent. It was Hughie's wife who alerted them to the fire in the centre, whereupon her brave husband ran to the aid of those inside.

The weather over the next day or two suited the sombre atmosphere that had descended on the Isle of Man. "The joys of a holiday Island had changed," said Roger. "It was a time I will never forget."[101]

Robert E. Wilson, an educational and employment support worker and author, from Northern Ireland, recovered quickly from the injuries he sustained in the fire, though the memories of that night are as fresh as ever.

A teenage Robert was enjoying a holiday on the Isle of Man before the start of his A Level year. He was on one of the upper terraces in Summerland when smoke began to appear. If it hadn't been for the rain, he said, then he might have gone to watch the stock cars in Onchan Park. Others did brave the rain, changing plans to visit the entertainment centre in favour of a night at the stadium.

A year after the tragedy, as Robert stood on the cliff looking down on the remains of the once acclaimed building, it struck him how fortunate he had been to escape with his life. He thought, sadly, of the people who had been seriously injured, the bereaved and all those who hadn't survived.

Robert feels very strongly that the disaster must not be forgotten. He often encounters people who know nothing about it. The name

Summerland has no frightening connotations for them.

Robert is vigilant about methods of escape in any building he enters. He remains uneasy in crowds. The sound of a smoke alarm going off, even when it is just a test, startles him. I understand that completely. When this happened recently, the person he was working with spotted his reaction. Robert explained about Summerland and how the effects of being in a situation like that stay with you. "Funny how just one thing can change everything," he says, about the tragic fire. How true that is.[102]

During a recent train journey, Philip Warren was unexpectedly reunited with the person who had been his best man. His thoughts turned to 1973, when he travelled to the Isle of Man with his new wife to do the same for his friend. The couple, who were staying in Ramsey, visited Summerland on 2nd August, where a lovely evening came to a dreadful conclusion. Thankfully, Philip and his wife managed to escape. They heard a lady with an Irish accent say there was a fire, whereupon they were able to leave swiftly and without injury. On the drive back to Ramsey, Philip stopped at the top of the hill. The catastrophic scene lay below. Almost five decades on, the memories are still as vivid, and the couple often think of those who weren't as fortunate, and of how things might have turned out for them.[103]

Several years ago, a Manx friend visited the Kaye Garden one afternoon, and discovered a lovely bunch of flowers propped against the central stone of the memorial. A card was tucked behind the flowers. I found the words written on it extremely moving. The envelope was addressed "To Connie Atkins with fond childhood memories." Inside, it said, "To Mrs S'atkin, Katkins. It took 43 years to reach you, but we never forgot you. Love from the two little girls next door, Beverley and Susan xxxx."

Constance Atkins, from Kimberworth in Rotherham, had not realised how serious the fire in Summerland was. She helped her elderly mother out, then returned for her jacket. Mrs Atkins, forty-six, didn't know, as she made her way up the flying staircase, that she was climbing towards death.

Ellen Palfrey, from St Helens, sustained burns to her arms, legs and face in the Summerland fire. The burns on her face were clearly visible in a photograph published by the *Daily Mail*, nine days later. Mrs Palfrey was transferred to the Special Burns Unit at Whiston Hospital in Liverpool, as were other injured survivors.

The fifty-eight-year-old lady had only been in the building for a few minutes when smoke appeared. "We decided to leave," she said. Soon, the place seemed full of smoke and flames. In shock, Mrs Palfrey realised that she didn't know which direction to go. Just then, she saw men breaking a window and ran towards it. Other people fell on her after she was knocked to the ground while making her escape.

Attended by two nurses, Mrs Palfrey smiled bravely while giving an account of her night of terror.

Sisters, Ann and Joyce Quirk, also from St Helens, recovered from their injuries in adjoining rooms in the same unit as Mrs Palfrey. Joyce, whose arms and legs were burned, explained how they couldn't breathe as the smoke in Summerland's Solarium became denser. The flying staircase was crammed with people possessed by fear. Amid pushing and shoving, some fell. For most, there was no helping hand, survival instinct had shoved sympathy out of the way. When the teenagers turned from the scene of chaos, to seek an alternative route, despair doused hope. A flame filled room spilled its panicked occupants into their path. There was nothing else for it, but to face the stairs again.

"I have never been so frightened in my life. I thought it was the end," said Joyce. Her sister Ann agreed – "I did not think I was going to get out alive." Ann had burns on the back of both legs, in addition to a fractured pelvis.[104]

Keith Jamieson was only seven when he witnessed the horror at Summerland. It was a popular destination for the family group, which included Keith's aunts, uncles and cousins.

"It had all the amenities," said Keith, "everything you wanted was there."

Once they had finished their evening meal on 2nd August, the family set off for Summerland, looking forward to an evening of fun. As they walked along the promenade, they spotted smoke, which Keith describes as "billowing" from the complex. Suddenly, the building seemed to burst into flames. "People were pouring out," declared Keith. "Some were on fire." The fire engines looked like "dinky toys" to the small boy, in comparison to the size of the building and the mammoth task they faced.

The family returned to Liverpool the next day, gazing sombrely at the scarred remains of the fun centre as they passed it by on the ferry.

The sights and sounds of that dreadful night will stay with Keith forever.[105]

Lyn was eighteen years old in 1973, when she went to the Isle of Man with her parents. She was getting married in a matter of weeks, and her dad was keen to have a final holiday as a family of three.

On the evening of Thursday 2nd August, Lyn's mum had a headache. Summerland wasn't far from their guesthouse, and it would be convenient for her to go back for a lie down if need be. Though they hoped she would start to feel better, then the family could spend the rest of the evening there.

Although old enough to drink on the adjacent isle,[106] under Manx laws, Lyn was limited to soft drinks. She sipped a cola while her parents had a lager; but after one drink Lyn's mum was feeling worse, and they decided to leave and go for a walk instead. Walking in the fresh air usually provided a bit of relief from the headache.

The three of them began to descend the busy flying staircase. Lyn found herself some way behind her parents due to the "platform" soled sandals she was wearing. When she reached the exit, her parents were already outside. As Lyn walked through the doors, she heard someone shout an expletive and the words "look at that."

Startled, Lyn stumbled because of her "clumpy" shoes. Gathering herself together, she continued down the ramp until she was in a position to look back at the building. A "sheet of flame" was streaking up the side. People began to run out.

Spying her parents on the opposite side of the promenade, Lyn hurried across the concrete bridge to them as quickly as she could. Her mother turned and vomited over the railings. White knuckled, she clung to the metal rail until her husband prised her away. Time seemed to have stopped everywhere except in Summerland.

Lyn described the scene as horrendous. The air was filled with screams of terror, people were wandering about in a daze, others were desperately calling for loved ones. Across the bridge, that Lyn and her parents had crossed, just a short time before, came the injured – those with charred clothes, with burns to their hands and legs and some whose hair had been burnt away in places. The little family couldn't bear it any longer. They turned and walked away.

When they reached the sunken gardens on Loch Promenade, Lyn and her parents sat for a while in shocked silence. Her mum took some painkillers, and when she was feeling a little better, they set off again. In a bar on Strand Street, Lyn's dad prescribed a medicinal whisky for her. It was an occasion when the rules had to be ignored. The young woman hated the taste of it and the way it burned her throat. Four and a half decades later, Lyn explained to me that even the mention of whisky caused awful memories to come rushing back.

Tired and numb, the family reluctantly agreed that it was time to return to their guesthouse. They had a long wait for a cab, as none of them felt strong enough to make the journey on foot. Taxi drivers had been taking the injured and their relatives to Noble's Hospital all evening – most of them without charging. "How lovely was that? For them to show such wonderful compassion," said Lyn.

When they arrived at their guesthouse, Lyn's parents retired to their room. The landlady was relieved to see the three return, they were the last of her guests to do so, and she had been very worried. She told Lyn that her fiancé had been on the telephone. He had found out about the tragedy on the news. Lyn could only imagine how anxious he must have been. After reassuring him they were ok, she explained that she would go into more detail when they got home. She couldn't bring herself to discuss it further at that time.

Lyn normally slept with the curtains and widow open, because of her claustrophobia, but not that night. A troubled sleep came to her in a darkened room, and despite the closed window, the smell of burning hung in the air, and beyond the heavy curtains stood the smouldering remains of Summerland's solarium.

On the morning after the fire, the curtains in the dining room remained shut. It was the final day of their holiday. On other holidays, that day would have been taken up buying gifts, taking last minute trips and having fun; making the most of the hours that remained: creating happy memories. They tried to do the things they normally did, but their hearts weren't in it.

"It was like being on auto-pilot," Lyn told me – "Doing things from habit rather than desire."

Although a decision had been made in the sunken gardens, not to talk about the fire; on that final day in Douglas, the tragedy weighed heavily on them. They agreed to talk among each other, then and there, about what they had witnessed the night before; but they would discuss it with no one else. Lyn spoke of the people who had stopped them to ask for details. That angered and upset her.

"We all felt guilty that we had escaped with literally minutes to spare, while so many were trapped." Lyn never stopped feeling guilty for surviving when others didn't. Although she travelled to the Isle of Man in 2013, with the intention of attending the fortieth anniversary service in the Kaye Garden, she couldn't bring herself to go.

The thought of what might have happened, if they had stayed in Summerland just a few minutes longer, was always on Lyn's mind.

In 1979, she and her parents returned to the Isle of Man. This time Lyn's husband was with them. They were drawn to Summerland. It was as if visiting the centre was something they needed to do in order to move on. This was a very different Summerland, externally, to the one they remembered. However, once inside the reconstructed building, which had opened again the previous year, Lyn felt that the bar they had gone into was too similar to the one they had been in on the night of the fire. They left immediately.

The Bradford City stadium disaster had a huge impact on Lyn. It occurred close to when her beloved dad passed away.

The atmosphere at Valley Parade was jubilant on 11th May 1985. The match between Bradford City and Lincoln City kicked off around 3:00 pm. Forty minutes later, neither side had scored, but alarmingly, smoke had appeared in the main stand. Flames soon followed. The commentary turned from tactics to the rapidly developing situation.

Almost double the usual number of spectators were present that day. Bradford City's considerable efforts had been rewarded with a third division championship trophy, which was presented before the start of the game – the last of the season. Television cameras were there to capture both the award ceremony and the action on the pitch.

Valley Parade, initially home to the local rugby team, was a year on from its centenary when disaster struck. When Bradford City Football Club was formed in 1903, the grounds became the venue for football matches too. The "basic" stand was replaced during renovations which began in 1908, and took around three years to complete. The new, considerably larger structure, apart from the concrete terraces at the front, seemed comprised mostly of wood: wooden beams, wooden planked floors, wooden benches and partitions. A wooden roof, insulated with felt and bitumen, provided shelter in bad weather. A considerable quantity of litter had accumulated beneath the seats in the stand – kindling for a giant bonfire.

A spectator inadvertently triggered a catastrophic sequence of events. The lit cigarette that he had thrown on the floor to be stamped out, fell through a knot hole and out of his control. The glow as it nestled in the deep pile of debris an unseen warning of what was to come. A slender smoke signal startled the man. He poured the rest of his coffee into the hole, and his son did the same; but it wasn't enough to divert destiny.

Wind fanned flames into a fury, and in less than five minutes the stand was engulfed. Scalding tar spewed from the roof. Fire spread faster than some could run. Escape was possible onto the pitch in the absence of a security fence, saving many. Police officers dragged the injured away from the blaze, their uniforms smoking, helmets shielding their faces. They were aided by members of the public. There were many heroes that day.

Concealed from the cameras, casualties mounted. Locked turnstiles created a crush. All but two of those who perished were fans of the home team. Children were among the dead. More than two hundred and sixty people were injured on a day that should have been a celebration.

When problems are identified, they must be rectified immediately. Warnings about the build-up of litter weren't acted upon. Fire extinguishers had been removed to prevent vandals from setting them off.

After the fire, smoking was no longer permitted where wooden stands were present. The stand, at Valley Parade, had been nearing the end of its existence when fate stepped in to hasten its demise. Demolition work was due to begin a few days later, to make way for a new steel structure. The tragedy led to improvements in fire safety at other sports grounds. Fifty-six lost lives initiated the changes.[107]

My dad took my cousin and I to a friendly match between Liverpool and Glentoran Football Clubs in the early 1980s. I could barely sleep in the run up to the game. Dad played for our local team – Downshire – until his back began to trouble him; but he remained involved with the club, and we would sometimes accompany him to a game. Although I enjoyed those occasions, they couldn't compare to the excitement of a stadium full of cheering fans and watching your heroes on the pitch below.

My desire to see Bruce Grobbelaar perform a handstand distracted me from my discomfort in crowds. I wanted play to continue forever on that spring evening in Belfast. The atmosphere was fantastic, and I couldn't wait to repeat the experience. Perhaps we might visit Anfield when my exams were over, I thought, as we made our way home. That would be a dream come true!

Though decades have passed, Saturday, 11th May 1985 – when news of the shocking fire at Valley Parade was broadcast – is as clear as ever in my mind. I walked into the living room to find Mum, who had been ironing, sitting in her chair with Dad standing behind. They were staring at the television. I looked too. I swallowed hard to quell the feeling of sickness. There must have been sound, but I could hear nothing but the pounding of blood in my ears. Then Mum's voice came, as if from far away, "Turn it off." There was no remote control. I closed my eyes as I bent forward to push the button. I couldn't bear to see those dreadful images on the screen; some were all too familiar. Dad spoke next, "I'm going to put the kettle on." Gradually, the hot liquid thawed the ice in our veins. The telephone rang; Dad answered it. A conversation that had nothing to do with tragedy allowed me to catch my breath. Mum resumed her ironing, but I knew her mind was on other things…

I went to my bedroom, to try to recapture normality. From my window, I saw children kicking a ball against a garage door a few houses away. The dull thud as it struck metal pounded my mind. They cheered, and I knew, without doubt, that I would never be in a football stadium again.

Carol, a nurse, lost her grandmother and great-aunt in the

Summerland fire. When she told me about her family's involvement, Carol was the same age as her grandma had been when she set off for the Isle of Man. A precious photograph shows her grandparents having a rest on a park bench earlier that week.

As a result of what happened to her family, Carol is cautious about the buildings she goes into, checking that emergency exits aren't blocked and ensuring that fire extinguishers are accessible.

Carol's aunt, Kathleen, spoke about the death of her mother and her father's sister at the unveiling of the new memorial in 2013. She found the service, during which the names of the fifty people who died were read out, very moving. Regarding the timing of the tribute, she referred to the "stiff upper lip attitude" that existed decades before, and the fact that people didn't express their feelings as they do now.

Kathleen was on holiday in Cornwall when she saw footage of the disaster. Watching the nightmarish scenes on television, she had no real concern for the safety of her parents or her aunt and uncle. Summerland did not seem to be the type of place they would have gone into. However, rain had enticed the two couples to seek shelter inside.

Harry Wilkinson had bought new shoes for his holiday, and they were pinching. He slipped them off to ease his feet while they were sitting on an upper terrace listening to the organist. When it became clear that they were all in extreme danger, Harry urged the others to go ahead, and not wait for him to put his shoes back on. Seconds separated life and death in Summerland. Mr and Mrs Thistlewood and Mrs Wilkinson made their way to a fire door, but it was locked. Mr Thistlewood tried hard to save his wife and sister-in-law. He was fortunate to survive himself, though seriously burnt.

Harry Wilkinson caught a last glimpse of his wife, sister and brother-in-law, in Summerland, as they made their way to the stairs. He survived by jumping over the bannisters to escape the flames.

Kathleen remembers her father telling her about the kind-hearted

message. I'd been asked to do an interview that would be shown on the BBC news in Northern Ireland. I had to say yes despite my nerves. I needed to show the people back home where Summerland was. I wanted them to see the beautiful memorial that Douglas Borough Council had placed in the Kaye Garden to mark the 40th anniversary. I hoped to convey the meaning of the sunflower. For some, who would be watching, the Island was a place where they had enjoyed childhood holidays. Perhaps they might recall those days and chat about their memories.

James Proudfoot, who would be filming the interview, collected me at the hotel after lunch. I had met his lovely partner, Amy Mulhern, a journalist, at one of the anniversary services, a few years before. It was cold that night, but Amy's smile was warm.

I was totally unprepared for the stunning display that greeted me in the garden. Every bed was filled with sunflowers! I began to cry.

When I sat in front of the memorial, surrounded by golden blooms, while Colin Cowie asked about my recollections of Summerland, I felt at peace.

Afterwards, James drove me to the site, and I laid a single sunflower where the building, that touched so many lives, once stood. Until then, I had only been able to observe the cliff face and the remains of the Aquadrome from behind a fence. I paid my respects to the past and begged the future to be kinder.

Paul picked me up at the Palace that evening, and we did an interview in the Kaye Garden before the others gathered for the service. It was to be shown in the new year. So much would happen before then; and the memories of that dreadful time have joined forces with those of the horror I experienced when I was five.

***

Councillor Ritchie Mc Nicholl has vivid memories of the night of the fire.

Ritchie and his brother had decided to go for a drink, and as they walked down Albert Street from their home, they were surprised to see many of their neighbours standing at the bottom, staring in the direction of Summerland. The young men were horrified when they saw, for themselves, the dreadful spectacle at the end of the promenade. Ritchie explained his reaction to the flames as a "chill" which coursed through his body.

The brothers joined the huge queue of people waiting to give blood. "The whole island pulled together," said Ritchie. Unfortunately, the pair were sent away because they didn't know their blood type. Only those who did were being accepted, such was the urgency.

One of his enduring memories of that night is the reaction of the firemen when they turned onto the promenade. He saw the looks on their faces as they realised the magnitude of their task. It wasn't a grass fire as some thought it may have been.

Ritchie is rightly proud of the new memorial, particularly, because the names of those who died are engraved on it.

Summing up his feelings about the tragedy: "It just moves you to tears when you see the age of some of those children that died and all the names of the people."[109]

Gill and John Skinner invited me for a cup of tea after the memorial service, during which The Worshipful the Mayor, Councillor Jon Joughin, had given a heartfelt address that included his own recollections of the tragedy. The laying of floral tributes concluded the event. Some other friends came forward to say hello: David and Luke Corkish, John Boyde and Noel McAteer, among them. It was wonderful to see them again. As we chatted, I was struck, once more, by how perfect the Kaye Garden is for the memorial. The Summerland site is close enough to be visible, but far enough away to take the sting from the night of remembrance.

The sea whispered as we climbed into the car, and gulls, like little ghosts swooped low in search of supper. I was introduced to Cassie,

Gill and John's enchanting dog, and before I left their lovely home, Gill presented me with some beautiful hand-crafted sunflowers. They have a very special place in my heart.

Friday didn't go according to plan. As I was getting ready in my room at the Palace, the fire alarm sounded. I was almost certain that it was the wrong time for a practice drill, but my mind was unable to accept the alternative. My heart began to pound. I felt weak. My legs had no strength. I remained rooted to the spot for a few moments, before finally pulling myself together. It took several attempts to open the door because my hands were shaking. The corridor was empty. I was alone! Just then, a man came out of the room next to mine. "I think it's the real thing," he said. That was when I went to pieces. I couldn't remember which way he went or where the fire escape was. All my meticulous checks, during the times I'd stayed there before, had been in vain. As I stood trembling, resigned to my fate, two members of the housekeeping staff appeared. Those kind ladies helped me down a flight of stairs that seemed never-ending. They calmed my fears by explaining that the alarm might have been triggered by something as simple as a guest spraying hairspray beneath a smoke detector. I apologised for my reaction and explained the reason for my distress.

At last we were out in the fresh air, where guests and staff had assembled at the appropriate points. Another member of the Palace staff, Irene Moffett, appeared to my right. She told me that she had also been in Summerland on the night of the fire! Her presence soothed me. She understood! Irene (who has become a dear friend) took me to the hotel foyer, where a tray of tea and biscuits was placed in front of us. The manager offered me a meal and could not have done more to ensure my comfort. Irene sat with me, and we chatted about our terrifying experience in 1973, and the effect it had on us. I began to relax. I could see that I had nothing to fear. Everything possible had been done to safeguard staff and guests alike. I thought of the time there had been a fire at the Palace, just months after

Summerland, and about how well the situation was handled then too. I knew that should the alarm go off again, unexpectedly, I had nothing to fear. I would be safe at the Palace Hotel.

I put off my planned visit to the Manx Museum, and settled down to a quiet afternoon catching up on emails and answering messages of support. Gill's flowers sat next to my bed, beside the other treasures from my trip, including a beautiful sunflower given to me by Murray Jones, the night before, and a framed print of Derby Castle in the old days – when no one could have imagined a building like Summerland in its place. Robert Farrer brought tears to my eyes when he placed it in my hands before the service in the garden began. Dear Rob, who I first met in 2013, at the unveiling of the new memorial. We were both in tears then as he told me that he'd never forgotten us: the people caught up in the tragedy – words that I'd longed to hear!

The phone rang. It was my journalist friend Francois, who writes for the *Banbridge Chronicle*. I told him about my surprise at discovering the Kaye Garden filled with sunflowers, barely letting him get a word in edgeways – as usual! It was just so lovely to be speaking to him from the Isle of Man. Golden light bathed the room, and contentment flowed through me. Suddenly, for the first time, everything felt right!

Chapter 19: The Best Medicine

Slender rays of sunlight slipped through the chink in the curtains. Behind them the balcony doors lay open, and a gentle breeze nudged me awake, urging me to get up so as not to waste a second of the beautiful summer day.

Gazing across Douglas Bay, where gulls swooped on the shimmering water and a visiting boat bobbed gently in the distance, I was filled with a sense of well-being. The months leading up to my trip had been difficult, and my energy level was low as a result. Since arriving on the Island, I'd noticed a significant improvement, though I still had a way to go before I could say I was back to normal.

I spent a few hours, after breakfast, in the Manx Museum Library – one of my favourite places. I find the cool interior soothing. A short while after my final trip to the Island in 2018, I received a wonderful surprise in the post. Following the pattern of my life, euphoria's stay was brief. Disaster was waiting impatiently to take its place. I haven't been able to use my cherished Library membership card yet, but I'm looking forward to a day when I can.

The sun was high in the sky, when I arrived at a packed Noble's Park. It beamed down on those gathered for the afternoon's activities, perfect weather for the fun day. Although I'd heard the park mentioned on many occasions, it was my first visit.

I had arranged to meet Malissa Cain and her children at the event organised by Douglas Borough Council. We'd been exchanging messages, and I was looking forward to chatting in person. Malissa is the daughter of late Councillor and former Mayor of Douglas, Stanley Colvin (Stan) Cain. I was very sorry to hear of his death, as the result of an accident in 2016; and that the family had suffered further heartache when his dear wife Sheila passed away the following year. The couple had worked tirelessly to raise funds for several charities, including Cruse Bereavement Care, during their time as mayor and mayoress. Malissa continues to raise funds in their memory.

I left Malissa to say hello to some of the councillors, who were organising the children's races. To my great delight, Council leader David Christian, handed me a fluorescent vest, and I took up a position at the finishing line. Laden with medals, certificates and sweets, I spent a thoroughly enjoyable afternoon handing the appropriate prizes to David's partner Murray, who presented them to the winners. Small hands tapped me tentatively, and polite requests were made for an extra lolly for a younger sibling.

While waiting for the little competitors to cross the line, I looked across the immaculately kept grounds and thought of the man in whose honour the park was named.

"The Isle of Man had never before seen, and is unlikely ever to see again, such a generous public benefactor."

Henry Bloom Noble (Bloom was his mother Mary's maiden name) was born in 1816, in Clifton, Westmoreland. When he was nineteen years old, Henry travelled to the Island, accompanied by his mother, to take up a position with wine merchant Alexander Spittall.

An astonishing change in Henry's fortunes was evident by the time he was twenty-four. By then, he had established a firm in competition with that which had given him his start in the business. At the age of forty, Henry Noble was "the richest man on the Island," having also made money in banking, property investments and shipping. He married several years later, and the newly-weds set up home at Athol Terrace, before purchasing the beautiful Villa Marina. Sadly, the couple weren't blessed with children.

Henry Noble died in May 1903 and was buried in New Braddan Cemetery. After dealing with specific requests, the trustees of his fortune distributed large sums to facilitate various ventures in Douglas and other parts of the Island. St Ninian's Church, funded by Noble's estate, was built in 1913 on land that he had owned. Education and Agriculture benefitted too. A School of Domestic Science and an "experimental farm" at Knockaloe, were fruits of his success. Douglas Soup Dispensary had a new home on Myrtle Terrace, thanks to Henry Noble. A hot meal, served at midday, would make the misery of the cold winter months more tolerable for the town's poorer residents.

Money from the trust enabled Douglas Corporation to give the Victoria Baths a major overhaul. They had purchased the Baths, originally part of a group of buildings, in the early 1900s. The complex included a hotel, shops, theatre, music hall and even an aquarium! It was a proud moment when the revamped premises, newly named, Noble's Baths, opened in July 1908. But things can't stay the same forever, and change came at the end of the 1960s, in the form of the Aquadrome, which, like its neighbour, proved popular with Islanders and holiday makers alike.

A new Noble's hospital was built on Westmoreland Road. It opened in 1912. Henry's wife Catherine, known for her patronage of those less fortunate, had provided the site and funding for the original Noble's Hospital on Crellin's Hill. It was Mrs Noble's wish that this much needed building was erected, but, unfortunately, she passed away before its opening in 1888. The old hospital building, after lying empty for a decade, became home to the fascinating artefacts of the Manx Museum. Henry Noble's legacy also funded a cottage hospital in Ramsey.[110]

I had spent some weeks recovering in the hospital founded by this man's generosity and cosy afternoons in the Henry Bloom Noble Library on Duke Street, and now I was enjoying a wonderful afternoon in the park bearing his name. It made me feel incredibly humble.

I wanted that hot Saturday afternoon at Noble's Park to last forever, but like all good things it ended too quickly. I slept soundly that night and woke on Sunday morning with a medal clutched in my hand. When undressing in the small hours, barely awake, I'd managed to remove the ribbon from around my neck before falling asleep on top of the covers. It was placed there in a light-hearted moment the previous evening, a precious memento of a perfect day.

***

From my seat in the horse tram, pulled by Charles, I had a clear view of the sunflower filled Kaye Garden. There were several people reading the words on the memorial stones and others were admiring the vibrant blooms. It was a magnificent sight.

Sitting next to me, were my new friends, Maria, a fellow author, and her lovely husband, who, as well as treating me to my first trip on a horse tram, had just treated me to a delicious lunch in the Terminus Tavern.

While we were waiting to board the tram, I'd approached one of the horses, hoping to stroke his shiny coat. I quickly learnt that he not only had a strong body but a strong personality too. He turned his head away and completely ignored me. I had no polo mints! Maria gave me some of hers, and he tolerated my pats until they were finished. When I told him how lovely he was, he gave me a look which clearly said that he already knew!

Maria's husband pointed out the indentations in the road where the barbed wire fences had been, when the boarding houses were part of the prisoner of war camp; and I thought of Angelo Morelli and the other men detained with him.

After our tram ride, we walked to the Kaye Garden to take some photographs. A couple from Northern Ireland were looking at the memorial. We began to chat, and I discovered that they hadn't known about the fire.

The little white Manx cat, that I'd first encountered in the garden several years before, was stretched out in the sun beneath the beaming sunflowers. It was a lovely surprise as I was missing my own cats, even naughty Cushla, who had caused me to be late to lunch. A cursory glance in the full-length mirror when I was leaving my hotel room caused me to stop for a better look. I had spotted several grubby marks, almost like a pattern, on the back of my white trousers, which I hadn't worn before. On closer inspection, they were revealed to be small paw prints. I knew immediately who the culprit was. While I was moving from room to room gathering what I needed for my trip, Cushla had endeavoured to make herself a bed in my suitcase. I thought I had succeeded in thwarting her plans, but I should have known better! Maria had booked a table at the Terminus Tavern, and we'd arranged to meet under the big clock. I intended being early, but the last-minute change of clothes held me back, and I had to get a taxi. We arrived at the same time, outside the restaurant, and although we had never met before, we recognised each other immediately.

I had passed the stables many times, when walking along the promenade, but hadn't been aware that it was possible to go in and have a look at the horses. It was nice to see them in their comfortable stalls, with music playing in the background, on that glorious August Sunday. It was obvious that they were very content and greatly enjoyed being visited by adoring fans. Maria explained that they take part in ploughing matches in the winter, during which she and her husband enjoy capturing images of the magnificent beasts in action.

Maria and I began to correspond after she read *Made in Summerland*, and I read her first novel. This has now been joined by several more. They tell the story of how two of her ancestors met and fell in love against the odds.

On the night of the tragedy at Summerland, Maria and her husband were working on their new bungalow. In the light nights, they would try to get as much done as they could; and there was always plenty to do: coats of creosote to be applied to wood, bricks to be moved or stacked and all the many tasks, great and small, involved in building your own home. That particular evening, they were waiting for a man to bring a digger to make a hole for the septic tank. When he arrived, he brought not only the earth moving machine but the dreadful news that the big entertainment complex in Douglas was on fire!

The severity of the situation became clear when they looked towards Snaefell and saw a "horrid red glow" in the sky. The new home they were building was twenty miles from the Island's capital!

When I was working on *Made in Summerland*, my mother told me about the dance she and my dad had been to in Ramsey, while on Honeymoon. The dance floor was made of glass with twinkling lights underneath. After reading the book, Maria contacted me to chat about this and other coincidences she'd found.

As a single lady, Maria had an apartment in a house next to the Beach Hotel on Ramsey's Ballure Promenade. The beat of the drum penetrated her bedroom wall during dances, but far from being irksome, Maria found it exhilarating. There was a large dance floor on the first level, she told me, but the Ocean Bar in the basement was unique. It had a glass floor!

Maria also enlightened me about the location of the Sundome in Ramsey – the first on the Island – something I had been curious about for a while.

On Sunday afternoon, I went to look for the disused public lift that had carried people from the promenade to the Falcon Cliff Hotel. I used to gaze up at the building from my room at the back of the Palace and wonder about the lift, which fascinated me. My friend, Alan Spencer, had sent some photos to pinpoint its location, and I spent a contented half hour studying what remained of the cliff railway. I felt very emotional and full of longing for those bygone days on Mona's Isle.

That wonderful Sunday ended, and I slept dreamlessly as time swiftly passed. I wish I had known, then, what the future had in store for me. I might have stayed awake and savoured those precious hours while looking out at Douglas Bay, as I'd often done before because there is nowhere in the world I'd rather be.

At the airport, I chatted to a couple who were also returning to Northern Ireland. During the conversation they asked the nature of my trip – did I have family on the Isle of Man or was I there on holiday? I explained about travelling to the Island every August for the anniversary. They said the tragedy reminded them of the fatal fire at Maysfield Leisure Centre in Belfast.

The centre, also a popular venue for concerts and boxing matches, closed for good in 2004, twenty years after the fire that claimed six lives.

I'm sure, like me, many people recall being sent to fetch equipment from the storeroom in the school gym. There were several occasions, when some of my classmates and I rummaged around in the stuffy, windowless room for balls and racquets or mats, which we had to drag out. I still remember the smell of the mats.

At Maysfield, a fire started in a storeroom, developing unseen until it spread to the corridor, filling the building with smoke. Gym mats smouldered, giving off toxic fumes. In the panic, a sixteen-year-old youth went the wrong way. He did not survive. Two people who had been enjoying a game of squash on that Saturday afternoon, also perished. The other victims were a young mother and her little girls, aged seven and nine.

Although the smell of smoke lingered, there was no structural damage, but it was quite a while before the centre opened its doors to the public again.[111]

On board the *Flybe* flight, I settled into my aisle seat. The lady next to me admired the sunflower brooch in my lapel and began to talk about the interview she'd heard on the radio, not realising at first that it was me she had been listening to.

We were totally absorbed in our conversation and didn't realise that the flight attendant had begun the safety demonstration. I was suitably reprimanded, being in plain view. I felt guilty that I had been disturbing the other passengers during something so important; but when she turned away, those closest to me smiled, and one lady giggled. Despite the solemnity of the subject we'd been discussing, my neighbour and I giggled too. It wasn't the first time in my life that I'd been told off for chatting too much! I had absolutely no idea that a few months later, my ability to communicate through speech would be severely threatened.

Chapter 20: Borrowed Time

When my flight took off from Ronaldsway, in August 2018, I was happy in the knowledge that my separation from Douglas would be brief. Councillor Janet Thommeny had invited me to be her guest at a very special event.

The date on the calendar changed to 21st September, at last: the day I set off on my third journey to the Isle of Man that year.

Although a direct return flight was available, in order to get there I had to travel to Manchester first. I was worried because there was only a short interval until the departure of the connecting flight. If I missed it, I would also miss the event at Douglas Town Hall in the afternoon. Thankfully, I was feeling much better than I had been in June, when in a similar situation, and not overly tired, despite the early start. Everything went according to plan.

Janet had kindly arranged to collect me, and when I switched on my phone there was a message to say she was parked in front of the main doors. It was so nice to have someone waiting for me instead of going to catch a bus.

When we arrived at Janet's home, her adorable collie Annie greeted us enthusiastically. The hours slipped away as we chatted, and soon it was time to get ready.

It seemed surreal to be climbing into a taxi, dressed in our finery, on a Friday afternoon. The driver asked us if we were going to a wedding! How different it was from my usual afternoon at the end of the week. A black cat crossed the road in front of the taxi. I felt light-hearted and happy. It turned out to be the last Friday in my life that I would ever feel that way.

How wonderful it was to be reunited with the other members of the council and their partners. I struggled to keep the tears at bay during the speeches. We were surrounded by photographs of past mayors, some of whom I recognised, including Samuel Webb. I won't try to find the words to describe my feelings as I sat in the gallery with the friends and relatives of the gentleman upon whom the well-deserved honour of Freeman of the Borough had just been conferred: David Christian MBE, JP, leader of the council.

David is deeply passionate about Douglas and has done so much for the town and its people. He helped me to find a way forward when I was in the depths of despair. He gave me hope when I thought all hope was gone. I, too, am deeply passionate about Douglas and during my terrible ordeal, that, unknown to me, was only eight weeks away, I was distraught by the thought that I might never be able to return.

On Saturday morning, Janet took me to see the poppy bench outside the town hall. I'd spotted the eye-catching seat on my way in the night before, but it was dark when we left, and I didn't get a good look. Afterwards, we walked to the Sunken Gardens on Loch Promenade, where there were two more poppy benches, one on either side of the memorial to Sir William Hillary – founder of the charity we know as the Royal National Lifeboat Institution.

The impressive monument portrays the courageous Yorkshire-man and his team of volunteers, rowing through choppy waters to aid the crew of the *St George*, which foundered in Douglas Bay, November 1830 – one of many maritime rescues they were responsible for.

Two years later, Sir William had the Tower of Refuge built in the bay: a haven for stricken sailors. It marks the spot where the *St George* was wrecked.

It was through the efforts of Hillary, a British soldier who came to live on the Isle of Man, that the National Institution for the Preservation of Life From Shipwreck (the word Royal was later added. Its use granted by George IV) came into being. Three decades later it became the RNLI.[112]

The central flower bed in the gardens had a border that was

scattered with brightly painted metal poppies. A Manx triskelion stood out in the verdant bed; flowers bloomed within it. Most touching of all were the three silhouettes – the *Silent Soldiers*, heads bent in reflection. I gazed through the "ghostly" figures, saw the world carrying on as usual and felt a stab of pain for all the young men for whom there was no tomorrow.

Our final stop was Douglas Head, where there was a clear view of the Tower of Refuge – an outline of which appears beneath the poppies on the commemorative benches – It was a gorgeous morning; fluffy white clouds hung low over far-off hills, and the blue water of the bay was calm. William Hillary was dressed for colder weather. Clutching his long cloak tightly about his neck, he looks towards distant trouble – only visible to him. His boot clad feet are boat bound, face set against the wind, immortalised in bronze.

The Camera Obscura tempted me, but that was for another day, when all the hours weren't spoken for.

Janet explained about the huge poppy that was planned to mark the one hundredth anniversary of the end of World War One. The ground was already prepared to receive the giant flower, which would be floodlit. A permanent tribute to all those who served their country so bravely. One thousand, one hundred and sixty-five Manx men didn't come home.

On Saturday evening, we attended the Mayor's charity event – a meal on board the steam train that travelled from Douglas to Castletown. Janet treated me to a ticket, and I had been looking forward to the adventure.

A warm welcome was waiting at the station. The Mayor and Mayoress, Jon and Angela Joughin had worked extremely hard, and the evening was a huge success.

When climbing on board the train, images from a childhood trip to Shane's Castle, in Antrim, had flooded my mind. The shrill whistle startled me that day, and the gush of steam was alarming, but I was safe next to Grandad, whose eyes were alight. It made me happy to see him that way, as his face was usually composed. He rarely went out, except to work, but trains were his passion. He wouldn't miss an opportunity to take photographs that would later be turned into slides. I loved to see him carrying the projector from his room and the screen that rolled down like a blind. The click of the machine, as the next image loaded, was pleasing, and we laughed if it was the wrong way round. Grandad's camera is mine now. Once in a while, I take it from the box that stores a lifetime of cherished mementoes. I still see his hands holding it steady, to ensure the perfect shot. Sensitive hands that fixed delicate parts to model aeroplanes and put together the footery insides of a clock. Gentle hands that soothed injured animals but were capable of hard work as well. Hands that guided two little girls. Hands that stopped moving too soon.

Midway to our destination, the train was halted for the main course to be served. I was impressed, once again, by the superb food. A buffet reception at the station had also been delicious. The quality of Manx produce is outstanding. The spot the train stopped at afforded us a stunning sea view. I thought of my parents, who had travelled on the steam train several times, and of how they had enjoyed those journeys. I decided I would return the following year, with Mum, but that dream disintegrated into dust, just a few months later; and the particles drifted off beyond reach.

Janet pointed out places of interest, and I was reminded of the connection that *Thomas the Tank Engine* and his friends have with the Island. When I decorated my son's bedroom with images of the colourful engines, many years ago, I had no idea that the author was inspired by the diocese of Sodor and Man. Perhaps, one day, my grandsons will ride on the steam train and think of the Reverend W. Awdry: creator of those little characters – so much a part of their young lives.

A short stop in Castletown allowed us to stretch our legs. As we made our way for coffee another black cat appeared, winding around our legs for attention: it was the third one we had seen that day. It must surely be a good omen, I decided.

While we travelled back to Douglas, desserts were served. Then, the raffle was drawn.

The black cats did indeed prove lucky. It turned out that I had several winning tickets – unusual for me. My only success, prior to this, was receiving a prize from Blue Peter – a Rupert Bear annual for guessing the number of squares on the little bear's scarf. It's still in the padded envelope it arrived in, with a note of congratulations tucked inside; perfectly preserved for four decades. I enjoyed walking along the rocking carriages to fetch my prizes. It is a memory I hold very dear, because it's something that I couldn't do now.

I met up with Andy Kneale on Sunday. We enjoyed a Costa coffee in the sea terminal and chatted about the book. Andy, a keen pool player, had a stroke in his early twenties, but overcame the challenges that presents. His courage, positivity and enthusiasm are inspiring, and I was sad when we had to part. I hoped that we could meet again, but the fates had other plans!

My original intention had been to have an early night ahead of my trip home, but I was restless and full of energy. I *had* to go out! Inevitably, my feet led me to the northern end of the promenade. I stood for a moment at the fork in the road, deciding which direction to take.

A new sign changed colours above the arched entrance to Summerhill Glen. I traced the words on the plaque fixed to the wall with my finger, before going into that magical place – the "Fairy Glen" of my childhood.

At the top of the steps, I encountered a young police officer, who had been checking that all was well. We chatted for a while, and he told me how he was looking forward to bringing his little girl to see the illuminations, when she was old enough to understand. His words caused me to grieve for the loss of my father, whose wish had been granted, but with tragedy following closely behind.

I explored every inch of the glen that night. Tiredness seemed an alien thing. I was loath to leave. Halfway down Summer Hill, I stopped and looked back. I must have known, somehow, that from then on, I would only see the glen in my dreams.

Everything drew my attention during that final evening in Douglas. The little ticket office of the MER – the gingerbread house of my youth – seemed to glow in the streetlights. Behind it, the horse tram depot appealed for notice. Almost twelve decades old, it was on borrowed time too. A while ago, it seemed that both horses and trams might find a new home on the derelict Summerland site albeit a temporary one.

A gate near the Terminus Tavern was open. I hadn't expected that. A sense of urgency came over me.

I walked the perimeter of the site, then set off for a second time. When I reached the point where I believed we had been admiring the view on the night of the fire, I stopped. Though of course we were at a much greater height, then. When walking, I'd kept my eyes firmly on the ground, but finally, it was time to do something I had needed to do for so long. Slowly, I raised my head and looked across the bay, not from the derelict site but from Summerland as it used to be.

It was tranquil in the garden, as always. The statue of Sir Hall Caine, by talented artist Bryan Kneale, stirred memories. Tired, at last, I sat down on the longer of the two sunflower seats.

A church, in our village, was the first place I had seen a bench adorned with poppies. How beautiful one would look in the Kaye Garden with a sunflower theme, I thought. I chatted about it on Facebook with my Manx friend, Susanne Dougherty, and she put the idea forward for consideration. Some time later, I saw photos that had been posted by Island Iron Craft on their social media page. Two stunning benches with big vivid sunflowers beamed from my phone screen, thawing the icy January gloom. I wondered who they were for. Not for a moment, did I dare to believe they might be for the Kaye Garden, but they were! I longed to travel to Douglas to see them, but I had to wait. August seemed ages away. However, an opportunity came sooner than I expected.

In June 2018, when I travelled to the Island to be interviewed for *The Fires That Foretold Grenfell*, I stayed at the Empress Hotel. My old home still felt the same, to my great relief. I had been worried that I would find it changed.

Jamie Roberts, of Amos Pictures, collected me at the hotel, and I enjoyed the drive to Kirk Michael, where he was staying with the rest of the team. Josh Clague and his friend, Joe, arrived after the interview – just the right time for a cup of tea! The young Manx men were working on a documentary about the disaster themselves, and when we'd finished our drink we set off for Douglas and the iMuseum. Josh interviewed me in the room I first visited in 2014. My life would be very different when I returned to that room again.

Alan Christian and his lovely wife came to the Empress to say hello. We were joined by John Boyde. It was so nice to meet them all in person: something I hadn't expected when I wrote to six of the firefighters who had attended the blaze in Summerland.

I met Godfrey when I was staying with Janet in September. We had chatted at length on the phone after he received my letter, but his visit was completely unexpected – another wonderful surprise!

It was raining on the eve of the first anniversary of the Grenfell fire, dashing my hope of seeing the new benches in the sunshine. Typical, I thought, as there had been a long dry spell. But, if I didn't go then, I would have to wait until August, and I couldn't bear that! I asked the lady on reception to call a taxi while I went to fetch a jacket. The driver was full of craic, and when we pulled up outside the garden, he said he would wait, for which I was very grateful.

They were stunning!

I bent forward to touch one of the sunflowers. Raindrops ran off the hood of my yellow raincoat and into my eyes, blurring my vision, but it didn't matter. I could still see them clearly in my heart.

A sea breeze roused me from my reverie. It was growing colder, a reminder that autumn was well established. I wondered again at the paradox of the season: decay and incredible beauty. Withered petals lined the beds – all that remained of the glorious summer display.

The words of a Rupert Brooke poem, *The Soldier*, drifted into my mind…

Forever Summer

In Doolish, Ellan Vannin,
There's a road called Summer Hill.
At its foot, a little garden,
Where time stands still.

Each second day of August,
The air is filled with scent,
From flowers laid in tribute
To a very sad event.

The petals are so pretty.
But their lives are very brief.
Decay soon makes a pattern
On each and every leaf.

Now, sunflowers bloom there always
In that place of memories dear.
To give rest to all who travel,
From whether far or near.

Those golden treasures radiate
Their light to heaven above.
They symbolise remembrance
and a deep abiding love.

No matter what the weather brings
To Mona's fairy shore, [113]
In a quiet little haven
'Twill be summer ever more.

We Will Not Forget

Frederick John Allen (60)
Frances Mary Allen (54)
Constance Atkins (46)
William Stuart Aves (18)
Anne Barber (69)
Alan Barker (20)
James Hewitt Bramhall Bennett (43)
Beryl Bennett (41)
Mary Sarah Boyd (45)
Thomas Brady (44)
Catherine Brady (43)
Mabel Alice Buckeldee (59)
John Millar Carson (62)
Richard Cheetham (52)
Elizabeth Cheetham (52)
June Cheetham (13)
Frederick William Glayzer (49)
Olive Bertha Glayzer (49)
Andrea Margaret Glayzer (13)
William Henry Goldsmith (62)
Phoebe Goldsmith (60)
William Robert Hamilton (30
Beryl Ann Hendrick (32
Anastasia Hughes (48
Marcia Hughes (58
Stanley Wyllie Kellet (37
Sean Terence Kelly (21
Allison Little (35)
Keith Baldwin Maceachern (23)
Hubert James Manning (57)

Gladys Mary Manning (55)
Elizabeth McKenzie (70)
Betty Ann Moulds (34)
Beverley Ann Moulds (12)
Debra Jayne Moulds (10)
Amanda Jean Moulds (10)
Lorna Bryson Norton (35)
Bernard Malcolm Ogden (41)
Margaret O'Hara (41)
Tracy O'Hara (10)
Julie Panter (14)
David Piper (17)
Dennis Arthur Sandford (43)
Elsie Stevens (68)
Alexander Gibson Stevenson (35)
Jean Davis Stevenson (33)
Jane Tallon (13)
Annie Thistlewood (55)
Kathleen Wilkinson (56)
Gary Martin Williams (11)

Epilogue

Christmas was five and a half weeks away. Although I usually put the tree up on 1st December, I had the urge, that year, to get things done early. The decorations, retrieved from the shed, were waiting in a dusty box to be exclaimed over. There were always one or two pieces that we'd forgotten about.

The dreaded vertigo spoiled the premature festive spirit a little, but the attack was short-lived. Worse was to come. Just before 7:00 pm, I bent down to pick up my phone, and as I straightened up a strange sensation came over me – a panic attack? It started off that way.

I was burning – my face this time, not my limbs. Suddenly, I realised what was happening. "Call an ambulance," I told my husband, who mercifully was at home that evening. "I'm having a stroke."

While the stroke did its work. I silently grieved for my family whose lives would be shattered by the shocking news.

I was alone in a world of pain and fear, for the second time in my half century of existence. Beyond that dark place, life was going on as usual. It was a normal Friday evening for other people. Words that had become so familiar penetrated the dense fog of despair: "Somewhere around the corner, all is well."[114]

References

1: I remember feeling something was very wrong as we approached Summerland, despite my tender age.

2: *Charlie and the Chocolate Factory*, Roald Dahl, 1964.

3,4 &5: *Report of the Summerland Fire Commission*, 24th May 1974, Part VIII – Origin and Development of the Fire, paragraphs 103, 104 & 105 (page 38).

6: *Report of the Summerland Fire Commission*, Part IX – Factors in the Spread of the Fire, paragraph 121 (page 43).

7: *Report of the Summerland Fire Commission*, Part IX, paragraph 127 (page 45).

8: *Report of the Summerland Fire Commission*, Part IX, paragraph 133 (page 48).

9: My father's words from the account he gave during the compensation hearing.

10: The Oroglas on the roof melted on ignition and dripped down, causing burns in some instances.

11: Jimmy Hicklin, from Douglas, "saw a man on fire, his hair and back burning. He was carrying a baby in his arms." Jimmy, who was injured in the blaze, had gone to the complex for a drink. The shock of the fire triggered his stomach trouble. I believe the person he saw may have been my father!
  Sunday News, 5th August 1973, published by Ramsey Courier Ltd, Parliament Street, Ramsey.

12: I wrote to Dr Ian Phillips PhD MSc BSc, School of Geography, Earth and Environmental Sciences – a teaching fellow at the University of Birmingham – in 2010. Summerland had been preying on my mind since my father's death. Dr Phillips gave me answers to the many questions I had.

13: *Report of the Summerland Fire Commission,* Part XI – *Conclusions*, paragraph 246 (page 77).

14: *Thomas Shimmin*, taken from *Manx Worthies* (Chapter 9), A.W. Moore, 1901 [isleofman.com]. The verse appears on the memorial marking the spot where *Tom's* house stood.

15: The Drinking Dragon (Buroo Ned) is a rock formation close to the calf of man.

16: *Kitterland – Manx Fairy Tales* (page 109), Sophia Morrison (second edition), published by L Morrison, Peel, 1929. Re-print published by The Manx Experience, Douglas, 15th March 1991.

17: *The Brig, Lily Story* – Port St Mary Lifeboat Station, taken from the London Illustrated News, 8th January 1853 [portstmarylifeboat.org.im].
   The Brig Lily Disaster 1852, Culture Vannin – YouTube, 24th December 2017.
   Mona's Herald, 29th February 1852 [imuseum.im].

18: Legend has it that a grave in the cemetery at Kirk Malew, in the parish of Malew and Santan, belongs to a vampire. Iron stakes at each corner, linked by chains, are intended to keep him contained in his final resting place…!

19: Hop-tu-naa (Celtic) is celebrated in the Isle of Man on 31st October. It marks the end of harvest and the onset of winter (Samhain, 1st November).

20: *The Wizard of Oz* (film), 1939 – based on the book *The Wonderful Wizard of Oz*, L. Frank Baum, 1900.

21: *Peter Pan* (film), 1953 – based on the play *Peter Pan*, J.M. Barrie, 1904.

22: *The Deemster*, Hall Caine, Manx Classics, Camrose Media Ltd, published by Lily Publications, Ramsey, Isle of Man, 2013.

23: *Thomas Hall Caine (1853-1931)* Knockaloe Virtual Museum and Archive [knockaloe.org.uk/hall-caine].

24: Bram Stoker Estate, *Bram Stoker's Life & Family* [bramstokerestate.com/life].

Springer Link – *Beyond "Hommy-Beg": Hall Caine's Place in Dracula* [link.springer.com].

25: *Made in Summerland*, Lily Publications, 31st July2017 – the story of how my family became caught up in the tragedy, the impact it had on my life and my quest for answers and closure.

26: Hall Caine, *Sir Thomas Henry Hall Caine CH KBE* [en.m.wikipedia.org/wiki/Hall_Caine].
   Thomas Henry Hall Caine (1853-1931) [isle-of-man.com].

27: *Manannan-Mac-Y-Leirr, Manx Fairy Tales* (page 179-181).

28: *The coming of St Patrick, Manx Fairy Tales* (page 20).

29: BBC NEWS – *Manannan Mac Lir: "Missing Person Alert" for Game of Thrones Sculptor's Statue*, 27th January 2015.
   Derry Journal – Manannan Mac Lir: statue by Game of Thrones sculptor back on Binevenagh, 27th February 2016 [derryjournal.com]

30: Facebook – Manx Churches and Chapels Group, posted by Susanne Dougherty, 7th November 2015.

31: Summerland was described as a "Trail Blazer." The choice of the latter word proved rather unfortunate.

32: 3FM – *Policing changed after Summerland tragedy* [three.fm].
   TVIM – *Summerland Disaster*, 2nd August 2013.

33: Information on the charge and subsequent fines is taken from the prosecuting officer's account.

34: Facebook, Manx Nostalgia Group, posted by Vernon Moore, 7th February 2018.

35: Departments consulted – Isle of Man Government, Planning and Deeds and Registry.

36: Isle of Man Government – *Champion for children and young people in care* [gov.im].

37: *Report of the Summerland Fire Commission*, Part VIII – *Origin and Development of the Fire*, paragraph 104 (page 38).

38: *The Telegraph* – "Hunt for 'furtive youths,'" by John Williams, Saturday 4th August 1973 (page 1).

39: Olga Gray read a verse from the poem at the memorial service on the fiftieth anniversary of the crash. *In Memoriam* was written by Kathleen Faragher in honour of the victims.

40: *A Christmas Carol*, Charles Dickens, 1843.

41: *Time to Remember* (Manx Radio) – *50th Anniversary of the Winter Hill Air Disaster*, YouTube, 25th February 2018. Sadly, the presenter, David Callister, passed away on the anniversary of the tragedy in 2020.
   The Bolton News – *Son's wreath memorial at plane crash site*, 11th May 2005 [theboltonnews.co.uk].
   Isle of Man Today – *The last remaining survivor of the Winter Hill disaster*, 3rd March 2018 [iomtoday.co.im].
   Winter Hill Air Disaster Remembered – MTTV archive, You Tube, 27th February 2018.
   The Bolton News – *The Winter Hill crash controversy*, 27th February 1998 [theboltonnews.co.uk].
   The Devil Casts His Net (The Winter Hill Air Disaster), Steve Morrin, published by Stephen R. Morrin, Stockport, 12th February 2005.
   Isle of Man/Ellan Vannin – Isle of Man - History - Black Thursday, 26th February 2008 [bbc.co.uk/isleofman].

42: The names of the thirty-five men who died as a result of the plane crash are recorded on pages 147 & 148 of *The Devil Casts His Net* and at the end of *Winter Hill Air Disaster Remembered*, where their ages and places of employment are also recorded.

43: *Europa Hotel Belfast* (History) – *Colourful past, bright future* [europahotelbelfast.com].

44: *Belfast Telegraph* – *Barry's Portrush sold and business closed, family confirms*, by Jonathan Bell, 6th September 2021 [belfasttelegraph.co.uk]
The popular venue, previously owned by the Trufelli family (opened 1926), has been re-named *Curry's Fun Park* by its new owners. It welcomed the public again in April 2022.

45: *Morelli Ice Cream – Ireland's Famous Italian Ice Cream* [www.morellisices.com]
Personal communication
Cento Anni: 100 Years of Morelli's Ice Cream, Daniela Morelli, published by Colourpoint Books, 1st July 2011.
Summerland was described as "*The first of its kind in the world*."

46: BBC News – *Mussenden Temple, Downhill House and the Earl Bishop*, 21st June 2011 [bbc.com].
C.S. Lewis's Ireland, 15th May 2016 [cslewisireland.wordpress.com].

47: Yorkshire Live – *Retired Huddersfield teacher recalls fire tragedy which killed both her parents*, by Andrew Robinson, 15th June 2017 [examinerlive.co.uk].

48: *Evening Express – Aberdeen Mum tells of her girls' fire ordeal*, Monday 13th August 1973.

49: Manx Net – *Castle Mona* [isle-of-man.com].

50: Manx National Heritage (Eiraght Ashoonagh Vannin) – *Three Legs of Mann* [manxnationalheritage.im].

51: *Douglas – Palace* [isle-of-man.com].

52: *School Days*, written by Will D. Cobb and Gus Edwards, 1907.

53: *Daily Mail*, Saturday, 4th August 1973.
  Daily Mirror, Saturday, 4th August 1973.

54, 55,56: *Daily Mail*, Saturday, 4th August 1973.

57: BBC – *Isle of Man/Ellan Vannin, Where the sun always shines*, 3rd April 2008 [bbc.co.uk].

58: *Fire Cuts Cost Lives – Why FCCL will keep soldiering on....*, Friday, 2nd August 2013 [firecutscostlives.blogspot.com].

Summerland Fire Disaster – Dr Ian Phillips, Chapter 1 [summerlandfiredisaster.co.uk].

59: *The Liverpool Echo*, Saturday, 4th August 1973.

60: *The Daily Mail*, Saturday 4th August 1973.
   The Daily Mirror, Saturday 4th August 1973.

61: Dr Ian Phillips PhD MSc BSc.

62: *Sunday News*, 5th August 1973.

63: *Isle of Man Today – Palace Hotel worker Noel says goodbye after 49 years*, 15th January 2018.

64: *Isle of Man Examiner (Brialtagh Vannin)*, number 4640, 7p, Friday, 7th December 1973.
   Nigel Neal: The Golden Egg Murder (1973) – Manx Murders, Keith Wilkinson, published in Edinburgh by Mainstream Publishing Company Ltd, 2003.

65: *Daily Record*, Saturday, 4th August 1973.
   Daily Star, Saturday, 4th August 1973.

66: Frank Keenan – Facebook.

67: *Report of the Summerland Fire Commission*, Part X – *Factors in the Loss of Life*, paragraphs 160 & 163 (Page 56).

68: *Daily Express*, Thursday, 9th August 1973 [summerlandfiredisaster.co.uk].
   Isle of Man Today, 22nd October 2009.

69: *Daily Express* – Father tells how son, 13, saved him from inferno, Wednesday, 21st November 1973.
   Daily Mail – Wednesday, 21st November 1973.

70: *Summerland disaster Isle of Man 1973* – YouTube, 2013.

71: *Daily Mail*, 6th August 1973.

72: MTTV archive: *Summerland 41: Policeman's Story*, YouTube, 2nd August 2014.

73: Manx Heritage Foundation Oral History Project: *A Time To Remember*: Mike Ventre, 27th November 2003.
   Isle of man.com – Top Award for Retired Fire Officer, 23rd April 2007.

74: *Sunday News*, 5th August 1973.

75 & 76: *Summerland Disaster Isle of Man 1973* – YouTube, 2013.

77: *Report of the Summerland Fire Commission*, Part XII – *Recommendations*, number nineteen (page 80).

78: IoM TV Archive: *Summerland Fire 40 Years On: Fireman*, YouTube, 30th July 2013.

79: *Summerland Fire Disaster* – Dr Ian Phillips, Chapter 1 [summerlandfiredisaster.co.uk].

80: *Warrington Guardian* – *Standing at the Gate*, 10th August 1973.
 Warrington Guardian – *Tributes to fire victims* – 40 years on, 18th July 2013.
 Personal communication – Christine Carr.

81: *Isle of Man Examiner*, Friday 10th August 1973.

82: *A history of Scrabo Tower* – *Guardian of the North Down Coast*, by Debbie Orme [scrabotower.com].
 Scrabo Tower – History [Wikipedia.org]

83: Waymarking – *Joseph & Sarah Kaye* – *Douglas, Isle of Man*, 7th April 2017 [waymarking.com].

84: *Now We Are Six*, A.A. Milne, 1927.

85: T*he World's Worst Disasters of The Twentieth Century*, published by Octopus, 1st January 1984.

86: Story Corps – *Maureen Krekian, Lynn Everett and Joanne Krekian*, [storycorps.org]. First broadcast on NPR, 6th July 2007.
 CTNQ – *Sad Clowns, Hartford Circus Fire Memorial, 16th June 2011* [ctmq.org/Hartford-circus-fire-memorial/].
 Hartford Courant – *Back to the Circus*, by Lynne Tuohy, Courant staff writer, 15th May 2004.
 The Paris Review – *Tears of a Clown*, by William Browning, 6th July 2016. [theparisreview.org].

87: *The Hartford Circus Fire* – *July 6th, 1944*, Personal Accounts [circusfire1944.com].

88: *The Hartford Circus Fire* – *July 6th, 1944*, Memorials [circusfire1944.com].

89: *Report of the Summerland Fire Commission*, Part III – *The Structure in Detail*, paragraph 41 (page14).

90: Chicagology – *Iroquois Theatre Fire* & Eddie Foy's Account of the Iroquois Fire [chicagology.com]
 Smithsonian Magazine – *The Iroquois Theatre Disaster Killed Hundreds and Changed Fire Safety Forever*, 12th June 2018 [smithsonianmag.com]

91: *The Sins of the Mothers* – Frank Delaney (page 454), published by Harper Collins, new edition, 15th March 1993.

92, 93 & 94: *Report of the Summerland Fire Commission*, Part IV – *Bye-Law Submissions*, paragraphs 52, 53 & 54 (page 18).

95: *Report of the Summerland Fire Commission*, Part XIII – *Recommendations*, number 15 (page 79).

96: BBC Two – *The Fires that Foretold Grenfell*, Amos Pictures Ltd, 30th October 2018.

97: MailOnline – "*Mama, I'm dying…*", by Arthur Martin for the *Daily Mail*, 1st April 2018 [dailymail.co.uk].

98: 5 NEWS – *Five-year-old Isaac Paulos's father Paulos Tekle at Grenfell Inquiry*, YouTube, 29th May 2018
The Independent – *Grenfell: Man contemplated jumping 18 floors while holding five-year-old son*, by Laura Parnaby, 20th July 2022 [independent.co.uk]

99: *Report of the Summerland Fire Commission*, Part XIII – *Recommendations*, number 32 (page 81).

100: *The Mirror* – *Summerland…* by Kelly-Ann Mills, 22nd January 2016 [mirror.co.uk].

101: *Isle of Man – Island of Dreams (a personal reflection)* Roger McCune, 2020 [imuseum.im].

102: Robert E. Wilson, Summerland Fire, Facebook Group, posted 1st August and 23rd August 2022.

103: Philip Warren – Facebook,

104: *Liverpool Daily Post*, Saturday 11th August 1973.

105: Isle of Man/Ellan Vannin – *Summerland: The Glamorous Venue*, 28th October 2014.

106: The *adjacent isle* is the name given to part of the United Kingdom by the Manx folk.

107: T*he Bradford City Stadium Fire 1985 – The Football Inferno*, YouTube, posted by The Raven's Eye, 7th July 2022.
   Fire Brigades Union – *Bradford City FC Stadium Fire 11th May 1985* [fbu.org.uk]
   Personal Communication, Carol Flinders.

108: *Isle of Man TV Archive: Summerland 40 Years On: Remembering Mother & Aunt*, YouTube, 2nd August 2013.

109: Isle of Man TV Archive: *Remembering Summerland*: Ritchie McNicholl, YouTube, 3rd August 2018.

110: Tynwald, the Parliament of the Isle of Man – *Henry Bloom Noble (1816-1903)* [tynwald.org.im].

Isle of Man.com – Henry Bloom Noble 1816-1903 [isle-of-man/manxnotebook].

111: BBC NEWS – *Fire Victims to be Remembered*, Wednesday 14th January 2004 [news.bbc.co.uk].

112: *Royal National Lifeboat Institution – How the RNLI was Founded in 1824*, [rnli.org].

BBC – *Giant poppy installed as permanent World War One "tribute,"* 20th October 2018 [bbc.co.uk].

113: *Fairy shore*, from *Ellan Vannin*, by Eliza Craven Green.

114: *Death is Nothing at All* – Henry Scott Holland. These words appear on the memorial to the victims of the Winter Hill tragedy.

Acknowledgements

My intention was to finish this book several years ago, however, fate had other plans. The road I faced, at the end of 2018, was long and there were many mountains to climb. My goal often seemed to move further away, and sometimes seemed completely out of reach; but along that road were people cheering me on, picking me up when I fell – believing in me!

Miles Cowsill, my most sincere thanks to you and the team at Lily Publications. You have been endlessly patient. Ian Smith, Camrose Media, I am indebted to you once again.

Dr Ian Phillips, I had no idea when I posted that letter twelve years ago, that it would result in a cherished friendship. I can't thank you enough for your help and support. I am in complete awe of your dedication to bringing the facts of the disaster to the world. It seemed as if the Summerland tragedy had been forgotten. You changed that!

My last happy memories before the stroke, are of my September trip to the Isle of Man. I would like to thank all my friends on Douglas Borough Council for making that trip wonderful, and for the warm welcome extended to me every time I visit the Island.

The support I have received through social media has been phenomenal! May I take this opportunity to express my gratitude to everyone who left messages, sent cards and gifts, took photographs of the garden and laid flowers on my behalf.

Heartfelt thanks to all those who shared their stories or contributed in any way. I know it was the first time some of you have spoken about your experience, and that takes great courage.

My Isle of Man advocate – thank you!

I have mentioned in the book, the firemen who faced the inferno in Summerland. I can't begin to put into words how much it means to me, to have met John Skinner, Alan Christian, John Boyde and

Godfrey Cain. It is the most incredible honour to have the friendship of these brave men.

There has been heartache in the years since I began to write *The Silence of Summerland*. I am so sorry that several friends have passed away without holding the book in their hands – something they were looking forward to very much.

Dearest Sam, I was overjoyed to learn that you had been awarded an MBE. How I looked forward to your emails, and what a comfort and support you were. I wrote Dolphins and Finchley in hospital last year, while thinking of your own challenges. I hope you knew how much it meant to me, to be entrusted with the story of your magical childhood trip to the Isle of Man. I miss you more than I can say.

A few days before Christmas 2019, I received a message from Councillor Debbie Pitts. It contained devastating news. Debbie passed away on 29th January 2020. She was the loveliest person and had the most beautiful smile. I will never forget her warmth and incredible kindness.

We lost Mum at the end of 2020. It was a surreal year. She became ill amid the Covid crisis and passed away just five weeks later. We are still reeling from the shock. I couldn't focus on anything for a long time. Then I thought of how she had begun to speak more readily about the fire. She had even asked what was in the book. The day I opened my laptop again and read the chapters that mentioned her, was one of the hardest of my life. As I changed the tense in each paragraph, I could barely see the words for tears. Our little family is without its anchor now, but I am so fortunate to have the support of my sister Lynda.

When travelling home from England, in December 2017, after visiting my eldest daughter and her family, I was overcome with emotion. There were smiling faces everywhere. People were looking forward to a reunion with loved ones and to spending the festive season together. I thought of all those who lost their lives in

Summerland – of the young girls who didn't have the chance to grow up and experience the joy of motherhood. I have been truly blessed with five amazing children.

Summerland was a name that was unfamiliar to them when growing up, now we can talk freely about it. I am so thankful for their love and encouragement.

Tabi Clements, you have lived and breathed The Book for so long! Chief maker of restorative cups of coffee, responder to numerous calamities (caused by my ineptitude with technology), advisor and best friend, a simple thank you is not enough. You really do deserve a medal!

Tyco Guy – people say you are a dog; but they don't understand that, to me, you are a real boy. Your life isn't easy – being bossed around by sixteen cats! Though, I know you get your own back by eating their food when you think I'm not looking! You have been my constant companion and consolation in the four years since my life changed completely. When I returned from my stays in hospital, and the many outpatient appointments that ensued, you cuddled into my side and waited expectantly for those words – we're going to do the book. Your contented sigh was the best sound in the world!

My dear friend, Liz, I cannot believe you are gone. You were so vivacious and full of life. I remember what you said to me after you read *Made in Summerland*! Perhaps there can never be a truly happy ending when one has experienced tragedy, but there can be positivity, and there may hope.

He who has hope, has everything – Thomas Carlyle.